Born A Healer

"A healer in every family and
a world without pain."

Born A Healer

爱

Chunyi Lin

with Gary Rebstock

I was Born A Healer. You were Born A Healer, too!

Spring Forest
Publishing

Published by: Spring Forest Publishing

ISBN 0-9740944-1-2

Third Printing October 2005

Printed in the United States of America

Book Design by Laura Johnson

Cover Photo by Gallop Studios

Cover Design by Jim Gallop, Laura Johnson, Gary Rebstock & Cyndy Strand

Illustrations by Chunyi Lin

Acknowledgments

Through a lot of hard work this book, which I have dreamed to have for a long time, is finally a reality.

I wish to express my deep thanks:

To my Masters and spiritual guides for all they have imparted and continue to impart to me,

To my wife, Fang, and son, Ming, for all their love and support,

To Mr. Liang Yongxi, my teacher, my mentor, my spiritual adviser, and my very dear friend, for all his guidance and support throughout my life,

To my students for all the joy they have given me, for the stories they shared for this book and for giving me the opportunity to share the healing energy of Qigong with them,

To my co-author for his loyalty, advice, and research, for all his hard work, day and night collecting information from my students all over the country, and for shepherding this project through to completion,

To all the wonderful people at Gallop Studios in Minneapolis who took the photographs for this book and its cover,

To Laura Johnson for all her efforts and skill in the design and layout of the book,

To all of the many others who helped make this book possible.

TABLE OF CONTENTS

Part One
Born A Healer

Part Two
An Introduction To Qigong

x

Foreward

I receive many letters, phone calls and questions in my classes from people about specific problems. They might suffer from asthma and ask, "Can Spring Forest Qigong help with my asthma?" Can it help with arthritis, with cancer, with back pain, with depression, or with some other problem? My answer is always the same, "Yes, it can." Many of these people have tried many different medicines or other therapies without getting the benefit they hoped for. So, when they try Spring Forest Qigong and it works for them, they often think it's a miracle.

Many people wonder how this can be possible. How can Qigong help with all these different problems? Especially for people raised in the Western world, it is easy to understand why they have these questions. Western medicine is wonderful medicine but it usually focuses only on the specific problem. Western medicine treats symptoms or syndromes. The Qigong approach to health is entirely different.

If you have a headache, for example, and you take a pill, it may help the symptoms go away for awhile but it does not deal with the source of the problem. What is causing the headaches? It could be allergies. It could be stress. It could be a pinched nerve. It could be many things or a combination of things.

Rather than focusing on each one of these things individually and independently, Qigong focuses on all of them at once. Qigong focuses on the source or sources of the problem not the symptoms. With Qigong you don't have to identify the specific source because whatever the source, it is a form of energy and in Qigong you balance all the energy in the body, not just some.

Let me share with you the story of one of my students. Several years ago a young woman named Stacy came to see me because she had breast tumors. The tumors were benign and were removed by surgery but kept coming back. Doctors could only offer more surgery. She was skeptical about Qigong but decided to give it a try.

Within a few weeks, Stacy's latest tumor was gone. She has never had another and it has been six years now since Stacy first began practicing Spring Forest Qigong. Stacy also suffered from migraine headaches and severe allergies. She never told me about these but to her amazement she stopped getting migraines and she no longer suffers from allergies. By removing the energy blockages in her body, balancing her energy and keeping it flowing smoothly, all of Stacy's separate problems were addressed at the same time. This is how Qigong works. You can read more about Stacy's experiences, in her own words, on page 212 of this book.

While Western medicine viewed each of Stacy's problems as separate issues, in Qigong we are dealing with the whole person; the body, mind, emotions and spirit as one interconnected and interdependent being. In practicing Qigong you are removing all of the energy blockages in the body and balancing all of the body's energy at the same time. In this way you are treating not just a specific problem or symptom but your whole body, mind, emotions and spirit – the whole person.

It is very common for people to come to learn Spring Forest Qigong because of one major concern only to find that other problems get better or go away as well. It is my hope that this book will give you a better understanding of why and how Qigong works so that you may have this wonderful experience yourself and go on to share it with others.

Born A Healer

Part One

Born A Healer

"A healer in every family and
a world without pain."

Born A Healer

SINCE JUNE 1992 when my life journey of America began in Minnesota, I have already taught thousands of people in America Spring Forest Qigong, and have already used Qigong to help thousands of people heal many kinds of problems. People travel from all over the country and around the world to come to take my classes or to see me for healing.

I really enjoy my work. When I see people smile and walk out from the classes or my office without pain, no words can reveal the joy and happiness in my heart.

In my classes or in my healing, people keep passing the message around, "Chunyi is a miracle maker. He is a gifted healer. He was born a healer." Sometimes people asked me directly in my classes or office, "Do you think you were born a healer?" I smile and nod my head and say, "Yes. I was born a healer. And, so were you. Everybody was born a healer." Many said that was impossible. But people who come to my classes, workshops or use my self-learning materials to practice find that it is true. It is absolutely true!

In the Bible, Jesus said that everybody could do healing just as he did. People may have their own faith or religion. Some believe in God. Some people don't. Some believe in Jesus. Some believe in Buddha. Some believe in Allah. Some believe in the universe. But, do you believe in yourself? Where is God? Where is Buddha? Where is the universe? The answer is in our hearts. Within us. Healing yourself starts from within and helping others to heal starts from within too.

When you first hear, "You can heal yourself. You can help others to heal themselves." It sounds too good to be true. But it is true. You have the ability to heal yourself. You have the ability to help others to heal. With Qigong, you can not only heal your physical body, you can heal your spiritual body, too. You can heal yourself physically, emotionally, mentally, spiritually, and all at the same time. This is called perfect and complete healing.

The ability to heal is a gift. It is a gift that everyone is born with. You have always had this gift and you always will. The ability to heal is not something you can go out and buy. You don't need to. You already have it. All you have to do is recognize that you have this gift and then learn how to use it. Thousands of my students through their practice of Spring Forest Qigong have already proved it is true and it has transformed their lives. It can also transform your life.

If you don't believe it, it doesn't matter. If you have doubts about it, that's OK. Most people do. When I first heard about this, I thought it was too good to be true, too. But through my practice, I saw the truth, experienced the

4

truth and now I totally surrender to this truth. Let me take you to walk briefly through my life and see how I healed myself and gained my perfect and complete healing, and then became a healer and teacher.

My Way to Qigong

LET ME START WITH my basketball story. I was a basketball fan and I still am. From middle school on to college, I either played on the school team or on the division team in college. I am not tall, 5-feet-7. But my specialty was three points scoring. After my college I was assigned to work at a community college and I still played basketball a lot. I had quite a few injuries to my knees, ankles, back and wrist from basketball. Once I even got my nose broken. But I still loved to play the game.

One afternoon I was playing basketball for fun with a group of people of mixed ages. When I got the ball and saw no one in my way, I took off as fast as I could to score. It was a breakaway move. I dribbled the ball towards the opposite basket and was going in for a lay-up.

If you've played basketball you know that the rules give you two-and-a-half steps without dribbling to move

6

towards the basket for a lay-up. When taking those last two steps you take long strides, moving out and up, much like taking off for a long jump in track. You want to cover as much distance as possible while springing your body up towards the basket.

I was just about to land with my first take-off step when all of a sudden an older man in his sixties, who was playing on the other team, ran out in front of me to block my way. He ran right into me. There was no way I could stop so I threw up my forearm to block. He did not know how to defend himself. When my elbow struck him, he dropped to the ground like a falling log.

If I'd kept going forward, my foot would have crashed down right on his chest. If that had happened, it would have been disastrous for him. So I twisted my body trying to avoid him and landed awkwardly on my right foot. My knee was locked when I landed and I heard it crack.

I had so much forward momentum that I sprang upwards and out towards the basket. Trying to catch my balance I landed awkwardly on my left leg, again with my knee locked, and I heard my left knee crack. My momentum was still carrying me up and forward and I came crashing to the floor in a heap. You can imagine how painful it was.

I had intense stabbing pain in both knees. I couldn't stand up. I couldn't walk. Two friends had to carry me from the court. The next day I went to the hospital. The doctor said he could not do anything except for surgery because the cartilage in both my knees was badly damaged. He said the surgery would be extensive and he could not guarantee the result.

I did not want to have that surgery. So, I tried other things. I tried everything I could, like heat healing, cupping, massage, herbal medicine, acupuncture, injection, and painkillers. But nothing worked. I just lived with the pain and could hardly get around.

Later on it developed into arthritis. My knees were often swollen up with great pain. I could not run any more. I could not sleep well because of the pain. Sometimes, when I was walking or standing, all of a sudden my legs failed me and I dropped to the floor. When the weather was bad, my pain got even worse. The pain was so terrible that I even wanted to cut my legs off.

One day someone told me that a very powerful, nationally renowned Qigong master was coming to town to give a workshop on Qigong. People said that many people, just by attending his workshop, had their critical physical problems go away, even with tumors.

I was born and grew-up in this culture, and I studied and practiced Tai Chi and Qigong, as well as herbal medicine and acupuncture. The Qigong technique I practiced was very helpful to me during very tumultuous and difficult times in my life. I had even used my skills with acupuncture, herbal medicine and simple Qigong to help others.

However, there was much about Qigong I didn't know then. My first Qigong masters did not reveal the true power of Qigong to me. They may not have known it themselves. Most Qigong masters still do not teach these very powerful techniques to any but a very few of their students.

So, I had never heard before that anything so powerful could happen that just by attending a workshop, your critical physical problems would be healed. I didn't believe this could be true. But, since I had already tried everything else and nothing worked, it didn't hurt to try one more thing. Besides, I needed a miracle.

I bought a ticket and went. The workshop was held in a soccer field. It started at noon. Fifteen thousand people were there sitting on the ground. The master talked seven hours, nonstop, no bathroom break for anyone. So you can see how obedient Chinese people are.

He talked mostly about how Qi, the energy in the body, worked and how to make it work, and then he told a lot of stories of healing, and how through compassion, kindness and goodwill we could heal ourselves. While he was talking, he raised and waved his hand gently from side to side and passed Qi to the audience.

Like most people there, I listened with my eyes closed. He asked us to listen to his words without hearing them, without paying any attention. That meant that we were to use his words and sound as music to go deep into the meditation. Surrender the body. Let the Qi flow in the body. Not try to control the energy. Just allow nature to nurture and heal our bodies. No matter what kind of Qi reactions happened in the body, just take it easy. Don't analyze it. Just let it be. That's what the master told us to do.

I sat there on the ground and listened and followed his advice. About twenty minutes after we started, my body started rocking from side to side, and backward and forward, and then after a while, my body started spinning, first slowly, then faster and faster. I got scared and tried to stop it. But the more I tried to do so, the faster my body spun. Then his words came again "No matter what happens, just take it easy. Don't be afraid. Any movements are Qi movements. They help to open the blockages in the body. They are good movements. Just smile and let it be."

I surrendered. I let it be. I was rolling on the ground

9

backward and forward for about twenty minutes. Then my body became very quiet. Then I felt a great current of energy starting from my lower Dantian (which is deep in behind the navel) traveling up to my head, coming down to my tongue, and then it stopped. My tongue gradually went numb. Then my throat started making funny noises, and then all of a sudden I burst out into laughter. I laughed and laughed and laughed, nonstop, very loudly. I could not control myself.

It seemed my body was not my body any more. My stomach muscles started to ache but I just could not stop it. That was the Qi reaction. I laughed like that for about half an hour. It gradually stopped. I didn't feel any discomfort. I just felt so comfortably tired.

I was lying there very quietly for about ten minutes, then I felt some funny feeling in my toes. It was an icy cold feeling. The icy cold feeling started from the tip of my toes, both sides, then inch by inch it moved up to my ankles, my knees, my thighs, my torso, my neck, and my head.

My whole body was as hard and stiff as a piece of rock. The only part of my body where I still felt something going on was my heart. I was nervous about this. I wanted to move my fingers. I couldn't. I wanted to move my leg. No way. I wanted to move my head. Impossible. My body was not my body any more. Then, I remembered the master's words, "Just let it be. Don't worry."

My body stayed in that situation for about one hour. Then I started feeling some tingly sensation in my toes, then my feet, then up to my whole body. The feeling was just like when spring is coming and the winter ice starts melting in the sun, so peaceful, so beautiful, and so nurturing. The feeling was not only in the skin, it was in the muscle, in the bones! No words can describe the inner beauty of the Qi moving in my body.

Now, I could move my body again. My body became my body again. I was so pleased with what I felt. Then some itching feeling started, first in my face, then my neck, then my back, then all over my body, together with great heat. The sensation was like you were lying on the fire. But the difference was, on the fire, you feel the heat, the burning sensation on your skin, but this heat was burning from the bone marrow out. I wanted to scratch it but I didn't know where to start. It was all over my body. It was extremely uncomfortable. It seemed like ten thousand spiders climbing in my body from the inside out. This made me even more nervous.

It seemed the master knew what was going on in my body. He said "If you feel great heat and itching in your body, that is the best time to open up all your channels. Bear it. Very possibly you will develop and open up more channels in the body. Your third eye might open, too. If you scratch, you will interrupt the Qi. It might take you another ten years to get to where you are right now."

I listened to him. I trusted him. He was an outstanding Qigong master. He had high education. He had done a lot of research on Qigong. He knew what he was doing. His master was the chief of the Shaolin Temple at that time. So I gave up myself again. I was sweating, bearing all these unbearable sensations in my body.

This lasted about another hour or so. Then my body calmed down. It was quiet again. I was so relaxed. I could see the sky and stars with my eyes closed. I could hear some sounds from the distance but I did not know what kind of sounds they were. For awhile, I was able to see my friends and family and many other faces.

11

In my body I felt a breeze sweeping through my bones. What a beautiful, wonderful sensation! I felt so happy. This kind of happiness was not something like when you get a birthday gift or pass your first driving test. This happiness was from the bottom of my heart. It was so deep, so light. It was simply the joy of life. This joy helped me understand that life is so beautiful.

Uphill and downhill in the journey of my life came a piece of beautiful and powerful symphony. It was so wonderful. You don't blame yourself or others any more. The long forgotten love, kindness, compassion, and forgiveness all come back to you. You feel so rich and meaningful inside.

The workshop ended at seven thirty in the evening. I did the ending exercise as the master guided us. Then I stood up. A miracle had happened! My knee pain was almost gone. I was able to run, to jump again! When I discovered that, you can imagine how happy I was. I was running and jumping on the soccer field just like a kid. After another two months of practicing what the Qigong master taught us that day, all the pain in my knees was gone and has been gone ever since! And, I went back to playing basketball.

To me, it was like a miracle. And, I wanted to know more, as much as I could learn, about this powerful, wonderful kind of Qigong. While I didn't realize it at the time, that experience would totally change my life.

My Healing Bonus

I was so thrilled that the pain in my knees was gone it was months before I realized that I was not only physically healed, I was healed completely. The depression, the anger, the emotional pain I had felt for so many, many years had also left me.

Because of this new Qigong I was practicing, I felt so happy inside. I became such an easygoing person. I forgave all the people in my life who had hurt me and my family. I felt so sympathetic and understanding of them. This was the greatest bonus for me! The real freedom is not physical but spiritual. I got the freedom of my soul!

When I tell students in my classes that I had depression once, they would not believe me. They said "You are so happy, so delightful, so positive about everything. How could a person like you have had depression?"

Well, here is my story.

My Terrifying Childhood

I WAS BORN IN THE MOUNTAINS of China and grew up by the ocean. My parents were mine workers. When I was five, they were transferred to work at a harbor in the town of Sha Pa, which was a fishing village. Both of my parents worked for the government, as many did. My father was made the manager of a salt making company. Salt was important in China and the company my father worked for was one of the largest salt companies in Guangdong Province.

My father had a very good job and was paid very well for that time. But, we lived in government housing that was very simple. It was similar to what you would call row housing in America. The houses were all built right next to each other and the street that separated the houses on one side from the houses on the other side was not much wider than a sidewalk is in America.

It was a simple two story house. The downstairs had a

dirt floor and was mostly a kitchen that we shared with the other family who lived in the house. Upstairs was a sitting room we shared with the other family. We did have separate bedrooms. They were very small, about the size of a walk-in closet in this country.

When I was in second grade, the Cultural Revolution started. This was a terrifying and disastrous time in China. Mao, the Communist Party leader of the country, wanted to get rid of all the people who had different political opinions. He started this so-called Cultural Revolution.

Good people went to jail. Teachers and professors were forced to work in the countryside farming (actually they used the farms as jails to keep watch on and control these learned people). Hundreds and thousands of honest and learned people were killed. Rich people, such as land-lords, were regarded as the most evil people in the world. The whole country had to rise up to "Throw them on the ground, and then put a foot on them and never let them get up again." That's what the government leaders told us.

The Cultural Revolution created great animosity and division in China as people divided into different groups. Each group or faction claimed that they were the only ones truly loyal to Mao. But they had different beliefs and they fought against each other. No matter whether they lived in big cities or small villages people did the same thing. People did not trust each other any more. Even in a family, sons, daughters and parents became enemies over night. The whole country was in a terrible mess.

We lived in a small harbor city and the same things happened to our village. The schools were closed. All the teachers were taken from the schools and put together to receive "cultural re-education", which was simply brainwashing. Those good teachers were now considered evil people. Different organizations took turns to target them, criticize them and insult them.

I could never get over the fact that one of my favorite teachers, who was the principal of the school, was dragged out from my class, while he was teaching, by a group of young people and beaten black and blue that day. His name was also Lin. Mr. Lin was such a gentle and caring man. I was horrified by what they did to him. They said they would come back again the next day to give him even bigger punishment. Their reason for attacking him was that he grew up in a wealthy family and was the principal of the school. That was all.

The next day, while we were still waiting for our teacher to come, someone came to announce the news that Mr. Lin committed suicide by hanging himself in his room. I don't know whether he really killed himself or was killed by others. He left behind two little children and his wife, who was also our teacher.

At that time, my father was the head of a sea salt company. He lived at his work about five miles away from us and only came home once a week on the weekend. The Communist Party asked people to devote all their time and life to work. Working for the Party was the most important thing. People should even give up their family when it was needed by the Party.

So, my father came home only once a week, on Saturday evening, to have dinner together with the family. On Sunday mornings, he walked back to work. My two brothers, sister and I, together with our sixty-year-old nanny, lived with our mother. Our nanny was a single widow who my parents wanted to help. We accepted her into our home like she was our grandma and she helped to take care of us children when our parents were not home.

My Father's Arrest

One Saturday evening, in the late fall, when we were having dinner, a group of people from my father's work, armed with sticks and guns, came into our home and took my father. They said my father was a landlord's son, a bad person, and should be put in jail. They tied my father's hands behind him and pushed him out of the house. We were so scared, but my father was very calm. It seemed that he had known this would happen for a long time.

My mother was crying, she wanted to talk to my father, but they did not let her. We could not finish the rest of the dinner. A few months later, they found out my father was not a landlord's son. Once, a landlord wanted to adopt my father as his son, but my father did not agree. They let my father out of jail and he was sent back to his work but he was not allowed to leave the company compound and could not come home and see us.

My father was watched all the time and I became the messenger between my mother and my father. My mother would write a note then fold it and put it into the bottom of my worn-out shoes. She told me that if I felt I was in danger, I should go find a place quickly and take the note out and swallow it without being noticed. I should not trust any people. If I did not see my father, I just simply returned home. I never gave the notes to any people, not even friends.

I was only nine years old. I did not really understand what was going on, but I saw so much no child that age should ever see.

I had promised my mother to do these things. So, every weekend on Saturday after school at three p.m., I walked five miles across the long dam of the bay to see my father. I talked to nobody. A couple times I felt someone coming to search me out, I quickly got into a bathroom and took out the note and swallowed it.

I did not always get to see my father. Those times I just turned around and walked back home. When I did deliver a note, my father would read it, and then burn it. He would write back and put that note in my worn-out shoes. He would warn me again with the same language my mother used. Each time, from the reactions of my parents' faces, I could sense what was going on. It made me feel very afraid.

My father told me after the Cultural Revolution, when I was at college, that he wanted to commit suicide several times. There were several times he was taken by armed men and held at gunpoint. They would order him to say that some person he knew or worked with had said something not in favor of the Communists. My father knew what would happen to those people and he refused to make up a story that would get them arrested.

That made the armed men furious and they threatened to kill my father. They would fire their guns at him and demand he do as he was ordered. They never shot my father but it was terrifying for him. One time, he told me, he cried the whole night quietly in his bed with the blanket covering his sobs. If someone had heard him crying, it would have just brought him more trouble.

Many times my father reached the point where he

thought he couldn't take anymore. At those times he really wanted to end his life. But each time, he said, he heard my voice calling him. So, he hung on another day.

Abandoned and Hunted

My mother was working then at the local government's office in charge of women's programs. She worked very hard and she got home very late almost every day. Half a year passed, and my father was still not allowed to come home to see us.

Then, one rainy, winter evening our mother didn't come home from work. Seven o'clock came and we still hadn't seen our mother. Then nine o'clock came, and still no word of when she might be home. I went to the office where she worked, but the office was closed. No one was there.

We went to bed. Our nanny did not sleep. She was sitting in front of our bed the whole night. At that time, we did not have too much space to live. Four kids slept in one bed. Morning came. We still had no news about our mother. One day passed without a word. Our nanny asked all the people we knew. Nobody told us anything. Three days passed. Still no news. We did not know what had happened.

Our nanny kept making up stories to comfort us. Until one afternoon, when we were home playing, all of a sudden a group of people punched the door open. The leader was my parents' good friend. Once, when she was very ill, my mother gave her all the money she had to see the doctor and helped save her life.

Now, this same woman with her brothers and sisters stood in front of us like a monster with an iron pick in her hand, shouting, " Your goddamn mother escaped. We can't find her. If we find her, we will kill her. If you know where she is, you must report to us. Or, we will kill you too. Understand?!" Then they left.

They acted this way because they hoped it would show their loyalty to Mao and the communists. By labeling others as enemies of the state and going after them they thought they would be honored as heroes by their faction. It was madness.

Within five minutes, they came back. They said we were bad people's children. We should not have a house to live in. We should live in the street. They ordered us out of the house. My nanny was not an educated woman but she was smart. Before they forced us out, she was quick enough to grasp a blanket and an umbrella.

We watched as they sealed up our small house. The wind was blowing with cold, evening rain. Four little children and a sixty-year-old woman huddled together, walking in the rain down our narrow street, trying to find a shelter. We found a friend's home. He was kind and brave enough to let us stay that evening. But six o'clock the next morning, the same group found us. They took us out of the house and warned our friend that whoever dared to take us in would be homeless just like us.

Once again we were on the street. Three days we were in the street with no food. Nobody dared to take us in or give us anything to eat. When we were thirsty, we went to a well to get some water or caught some rain from the roof. We kept asking our nanny where our mother and father were and when they would come to get us and get bread for us. She always could make up some very promising story to keep our roaring stomachs quiet. Sometimes she asked us to imagine chewing a big piece of chicken wing. Sometimes she told us a funny story and made us laugh. Now, when I think back on that time, I really don't know what would have happen to us without our nanny. She was our angel.

I was just nine. My sister was eight. My two brothers were six and four. One time, my four-year-old brother was so hungry that when he saw a piece of sugar cane garbage on the ground he quickly grabbed it and put it to his mouth. I said to him loudly, "It is dirty! Throw it away!" He looked at me with his little dirty fingers in his mouth, begging me, "I am so...hungry. Please..." I turned my head away as he ate it.

The third night came. That night, as we huddled in the street, a gun battle broke out between two different factions. We could hear bullets flying above our heads. Bullets were flying everywhere. All around us. Bombs were going off. There were explosions everywhere. We were so afraid.

We were running from one door to the other, desperately trying to find a safe place to hide. We found our best friend's home. They opened the door a little. As soon as they saw us, they said, "We don't know you. Go, go, go!" Then, they shut the door tight.

My brothers and sister kept asking our nanny why they lied and wouldn't let us in. She did not say a word. She just asked us to be quiet and led us away as fast as we could go.

During the fighting that night a mortar exploded in the house where we had lived just days before. It blew-up right in our bedroom. So, in a sense, we were lucky. If we hadn't been thrown out of our house, we would have all been killed. So, I think God helped us.

Later that night, we were all huddled together in the

doorway of a house shivering from fear. We were so scared. The door opened and a very elderly lady came out. Immediately, we recognized her. She was a landlord lady and we became even more afraid.

At that time in China, a landlord, someone who owned property, was considered to be evil. In fact, a landlord was considered the most evil of all people. During the Cultural Revolution, the country was told that everything belonged to the state, to the government. We were taught that all good things came from the government and that it was everyone's duty to support the government. All property was eventually seized by the government. No one was allowed to own anything. No one was allowed to be an individual or think for himself.

A landlord was considered an enemy of the state and was to be hated. If a landlord walked the streets, people would throw rocks and garbage at them. It's hard for anyone who didn't live through it to understand. But, at that time a landlord was considered a devil. So, when we recognized this woman to be a landlord we were afraid she would do terrible things to us. I jumped behind our nanny to hide.

Of course, this elderly woman wasn't a devil. In fact, she turned out to be our savior. She looked at us and said, "Oh, you poor little children. I know people say I'm evil but I won't hurt you. With all this fighting it's too dangerous for you to be outside. Please, come inside. You'll be safe."

So, we went inside her house. We told her we had no water and no food and hadn't eaten in days. She said, "You poor children." She went and boiled some water and made rice for us to eat. She made five pounds of rice with a drop of peanut oil. It was an incredibly generous thing for her to do. At that time, five pounds of rice was very expensive. Five pounds was one person's supply of rice for an entire month.

We devoured the rice. It was so good. To this day when my brothers and sister and I get together we remember that as the best meal we've ever had. After eating, we were so exhausted we just wanted to sleep. The landlord lady invited us to stay with her and we were just going to sleep when someone began banging on her door. Suddenly, we were afraid again.

Our nanny and my two little brothers hid in a pile of hay. Hay was used for cooking fires. My sister and I ran into the back part of the house into a storage room. There was a large pile of wooden beams on the floor, long beams, used to support the roof of a house. The beams were there to be used to make repairs. They weren't stacked up. They were in a pile and there was a little open space in the middle. We crawled in and hid there, waiting.

The beams were piled up behind what turned out to be a coffin. At that time in China, it wasn't unusual for elderly people to keep the coffin they would be buried in inside their home. We were hiding behind the landlady's coffin.

The elderly woman went to the door and was met by a group of people armed with guns and clubs. One man had a pickaxe. They forced their way inside and shouted, "Where are the little kids?" They used my father's name and demanded to know where his children were. They said his kids had been seen huddled at her doorway and then just disappeared.

She said, "Well, you know, I'm the landlord lady. I am known to be an evil person. Who would come to my house? You can search for them if you want. I'm old. I have my coffin already and soon I will die."

So, they looked around and when they didn't find us they left. But, they warned the landlady that if they found out she was lying they would be back to get her.

This terrible, evil person, this enemy of the state, this landlady, saved our lives and risked her own life to save us. I was only nine and my view of the world was totally turned upside down by these events.

All our good friends, people who I thought loved us and cared about us had betrayed us. They turned their backs on us and virtually threw us to the wolves. Yet, this horrible, evil monster, this landlady, risked everything to protect us. Because of this, the concept of good things and bad things, right and wrong were completely destroyed in my mind.

The landlady protected many people. Her property hadn't been taken from her yet and she had a large house. During the time we stayed with her, she hid more than thirty people in her house. Many of them hid in the back of the house, which was really like a storage shed or barn where animals would be kept.

Our Escape

EVENTUALLY, MY FATHER was given a little freedom and allowed to leave his company's compound. Once he got out, he made his way to a town on the other side of the large bay from where we lived. That town was controlled by a different faction than our town. The salt making company my father had once managed was now operating on that side of the harbor. My mother also eventually escaped and made her way to the same town.

By this time, the government had sent out orders for the various factions to stop their fighting. Several times a truce was called but most lasted only a short time before more fighting resumed. In our town, they called just a one day truce so people could get food.

My father was a very good man and had always helped people. He gave most of the money he earned to help other people. Our family lived mostly on what my mother earned.

After my father was allowed some freedom of movement, some of the people he had helped, poor people who had nothing, promised to do everything they could to find his children. While the situation in China was starting to improve, it was still very dangerous for these people to return to our town but they did. They came back and they risked their lives to find us.

They eventually learned we were staying in the landlord lady's house. One night a man we didn't know came to see us. We didn't trust him at first but then he showed us a letter my father had written to us. My father was a chain smoker and had a favorite brand of tobacco. It had a trademark that looked like a train and my father's note was written on this trademark. Then, we knew we could trust this man. (My father finally stopped smoking and drinking when he was sixty-five, after he began to practice the Qigong I taught him. I was very proud of him for doing so.)

We made a plan to escape and make our way to other side of the harbor and safety. We did it like this. Early the next morning, my sister and I left the landlord's house together. If there was no news by midday that we had been captured, then our nanny and my two brothers would leave. But, they would follow a different route.

My sister and I dressed in rags that morning so we would look like beggars as we made our way through the streets. We waited inside next to the front door for our father's friend to arrive. Then we heard a special knock. It was our signal to leave. We opened the door a crack and saw the man standing there. He turned and walked away and we followed him at a distance just as we'd planned.

He led us on a round-about-route winding our way

through the back streets of Sha Pa being careful to stay as hidden as we could and yet not lose sight of our guide. We needed to make our way to a house across town where a relative of one of my father's friends still lived. They had been told to expect us at a certain time. At that time, they were to open the front door just a little. We were to run quickly into the house and immediately close the door. Then, they would sneak us out the back and down to a boat.

To reach the house we had to cross the main street of the town. We had to pass by a fort that was right in the middle of the block. When we got to that point two armed men spotted us. One of them recognized me and shouted, "You're Shu Jin's kid. I'm going to kill you." Shu Jin is my mother's name.

The man grabbed his machine gun and pointed it right at me. My sister was holding my arm tightly and she was very scared. I don't know why, but at that moment I wasn't frightened at all. I just stood there and looked at the man.

Before he could pull the trigger, the other man stopped him. He put his hand on the machine gun and moved it away. He said, "They're just kids. We're looking for their parents not them. Let them go."

The two men argued and the good man motioned for us to run and run we did. We ran as fast as we could across the street and around the corner. The house we were going to was right there. We saw the door with the little red mark on it we were told to look for. The door was open just a little bit and we dashed inside and closed the door. A man was waiting and we ran straight through the house and out the back door into a sugar cane field.

We hid among the cane stalks and then made our way

through the field to the water where another friend of father's was waiting with a boat. After they exchanged passwords, we took the boat across the large bay to safety. The boat was small and the bay was treacherous. It was very large, larger than San Francisco bay. The wind was strong, the waves were pounding and the currents were treacherous. It was a long day. We left the landlord's house before six o'clock in the morning and finally made it to the other side of the bay in the late afternoon.

When we got there, we saw from the distance that my father was waiting for us with great pain on his face. We ran towards him shouting "Daddy, daddy, daddy..." we held each other, crying with all our chest. Everybody around us was crying with us. After that many days and nights living in fear and hunger, in the streets and in hiding, now we finally gained back our freedom and finally we could see our father. Crying was the only thing that could show our feelings.

We cried and cried, in the middle of the path. The winter wind from the sea was blowing hard. It was bitterly cold but we didn't even feel it. Father embraced us and we held our father. Together we cried. I do not know how long we cried there.

With tears streaming down her face, a woman friend came with some steamed bread and gave it to us. We took the bread, still sobbing, and put the bread into our mouths. During those days and nights in the street, my nanny often comforted us by saying, "Once we get to your father's place, we will not feel hungry." It was true. We had bread in our dirty little hands now, which we had dreamed of for many days and nights. It was so wonderful.

My mother was not there waiting for us because my

28

nanny and brothers had better luck in their escape. They had gotten there two hours earlier. My mother was taking care of them at my father's dorm.

After supper, we washed clean and went to bed right away. Four kids, together with our nanny, slept in my fathers little twin-size bed. We put a bench to hold our legs. My mother and father got back late and they sat face-to-face talking. I could not remember exactly what they discussed. But I understood what they said. It was not safe for us to stay there with them. They decided to send us to the countryside where my grandma on my mother's side lived.

They did not sleep the whole night. The next day, they asked us to keep silent about what we were going to do. When evening came, it was raining again. After everybody was asleep, my parents took us to a boat. A friend was waiting for us. We got on the boat together with our nanny. We were leaving our parents to go to grandma's, which was about four hundred miles away.

It was a dark, dark night. The winter wind was strong. The boat was not in good shape. It was small, not much bigger than a canoe. The boat had oars and a small sail. It was old and battered and water kept coming in from the bottom. It was raining hard. The waves were high and a few times the boat almost tipped over. But we had a very skillful pilot. Our nanny was holding my shivering sister and two brothers in her arms, sitting in the middle of the little boat. I helped to bail the water out of the boat. I never stopped bailing with my little bucket the entire trip. The little boat was struggling on the rough sea for the whole night.

Several times I saw the expression on the pilot's face that meant things were not good. I could do nothing but work harder to keep the water out of the boat, our life boat, which was holding all our lives and hope. The waves were so big, and the boat was so small. Even now, when I think back about that journey, I cannot believe how we survived that night. And where did I get the power as a tiny nine-year-old boy to work nine hours bailing water out of the boat? The only answer, again, was that God was with us.

Early the next morning, we finally made it to the other side of the sea. The pilot asked our nanny to never tell anyone that he was the pilot and to get us out of the town immediately. To this day, I still do not know who he was. I have always wanted to thank him.

We left the boat and walked with our nanny five miles to the bus station. We took a bus the rest of the way to where grandma lived. Finally, we had made it to the country and safety.

We lived with my grandmother in the country for more than a year before my parents determined it was safe for us to come and live with them. By this time, the worst of the Cultural Revolution was over. Some peace had been restored but there was still much anger and hatred and sometimes violence.

After the Cultural Revolution, I didn't trust people any more. So-called good friends turned out to be the ones who wanted to take your life. So-called evil people turned out to be your angels. What an upside down world! I didn't even trust my parents. In my mind, my mother had simply abandoned her four little bananas.

It was years later before I learned the whole story from one of my mother's friends. My mother and her co-workers had learned that day that a group of one communist faction was coming to seize them all. Had they been caught they probably would have been killed. So, they all ran away. They barely got away in time. There was not time for my mother to send us a message. And, she knew she would have put us in even greater danger if she came home that day.

My mother and the two others in her office escaped right away into a department store. They hid there for three days before they escaped out of the city to my father's place. Just ten minutes after they fled another co-worker, who was still at the office, was seized. He was beaten black and blue, and was vomiting blood. Then the people who beat him put slaked lime on his wounds, leaving him handicapped for the rest of his life. If my mother had been caught, she would have suffered a similar fate. When I learned this, I felt so sorry that I once hated my mother for what she'd done.

Healing in the Countryside

While I lived with my grandma in the countryside I learned a lot from her and others in her village about the healing herbs and healing hands. Quite often, when people in the village got a lump in the neck or breast or somewhere on the body they came to my grandma's house. She would use oil and her hands to massage and manipulate the area. The very next day the lump had often disappeared completely.

One day I twisted my ankle badly and it was very painful and swollen up badly. My grandma's neighbor came and asked all the ladies in the house to each cut some of their hair. She melted the hair in boiling peanut oil. Then, when the oil was cool, she massaged my ankle with it. The next day I was running in the field again with

31

my friends.

I knew a country healer who used a regular needle to pinch the eyelids of a person to heal a chest problem that was considered incurable. I knew a lady in the farmer's market who could tell what kind of internal problems a person had just by looking at their fingernails. I also knew a healer who used a type of life-threatening, poisonous plant, cooked with pork fat, to cure tough skin problems safely and completely.

I always admired these healers who could perform such miracles and wished someday that I could become a healer, too. That year and a half in the countryside was the only time I felt safe and secure until I was much older. I lived with wonderful people. I learned to fish and how to raise chickens and geese. I learned how to ride a water buffalo. I was a kid again

It was all good and wonderful until the day one of my uncles was arrested. Some local government officials came and seized him while he was working in the fields. He had no idea why he was being taken. They accused him of being a counterrevolutionary but he had done nothing wrong. They took him to farmers' market where he was to be buried alive in public.

My grandma did lot let us go to see what was happening. She was in deep pain. That evening all the relatives came to her house. They sat together in a circle. The men were smoking and the women were sobbing. But nobody said anything. I sat quietly in a corner with my sister and watched. The next day my uncle's daughter told me what had happened.

When she got to the farmer's market, her father was already buried up to his chest. She learned that his "crime" was that he had owned a water buffalo some twenty years earlier, before the communists took over, and had used it to plow the fields while others in his village didn't have a water buffalo. According to these officials that made him a "landlord" and all landlords were to be condemned and damned to hell.

My cousin tried to give her father something to eat but he could not open his mouth. He couldn't speak. Couldn't even take a sip of water. She asked him if he wanted to say anything to his mother. He simply shook his head and closed his eyes. Then, one of the government officials walked up behind him pushed her away and shot my uncle in the head with a machine gun.

My uncle was an ordinary farmer, no education, hard-working and honest. He never deified the government. He was always very obedient. How could such a person be a counterrevolutionary? He had done nothing wrong. He was given no trial. He was just tortured and killed.

After this event my life was not enjoyable any more. I had to be on guard all the time. Whenever people approached me and asked anything about my family, I had to be careful what I said. We lived in constant fear. We lived in hell.

Life as an "Undesirable"

EVENTUALLY, WE WENT BACK to our old hometown of Sha Pa and lived with our parents. My parents were still considered "suspect" by the communist factions and were not allowed to return to their former jobs. Anytime some communist organization wanted them, my parents had to go where they were told to receive public criticism.

The entire town looked down upon our family. None of the other children would play with us. Wherever we went, other children were allowed to hit us and insult us anyway they wanted. We were not allowed to fight back in anyway. Our parents warned us that fighting back would only make it worse. So, we just took it. We were allowed to go back to school but quite often I got home with my school bag torn, or clothes torn, or bruises on my arms or face.

The schools were not modern, nothing like the schools

in the United States. We sat on long benches at tables, which were nothing but long boards laid on support posts. The boards weren't even attached which would prove very painful for me.

It happened one day at school while the other kids were out playing during a break. As usual, I remained in the classroom studying. I had nothing else to do. I was sitting at my table doing my work when a group of kids, some in front of me and some in back of me, smashed the two table boards together catching me in the middle. I was severely injured by this.

It was also the last straw. I couldn't bear the abuse anymore so this time I fought back. I hit one of the kids in the eye. That night, the boy's mother brought him to my home. She yelled at my mother and me. She said my mother was a 'devil mother' who raised a 'devil kid' to kill good people's children.

She demanded my mother pay for medicine to treat her child's injuries. All he had were some bumps and bruises, nothing compared to what they done to me. But that woman stood there shouting and demanding my mother pay her five Chinese Yuan. It was an outrageous sum. Eight Yuan was enough to feed a person for an entire month. My mother, of course, was stunned by all this.

I hadn't told my mother what had happened. She did not know what was going on. She became so mad that she grabbed me and gave me a good hit. I did not cry at all. I only held my fists tight and just took it.

Later, when my nanny helped me to wash and change clothes for bed, she found huge bruises on my back and chest. She asked me what happened, then I told her the truth. The next day my mother took me to see a doctor. The doctor said that I was greatly injured internally.

Then my mother felt so sorry. She held me tight to her chest and cried and cried. I suffered from those injuries for many, many years.

Despite this incident I was allowed to continue in school and to go to high school. The insults and abuse never stopped. I was still considered a 'devil kid' by many people. I was seething inside but I focused on my work. I always got the highest marks in school and was even made a class leader.

When I was little I heard stories about Qigong masters and miraculous healings. I loved those stories and wished that one day I could become a healer like that. During the Cultural Revolution no one taught Qigong openly. The government did not sanction Qigong and anyone caught teaching or even practicing Qigong would have been arrested. I wanted very much to learn and finally I found my first teacher.

Early on in high school I met a man who was a Qigong master. He agreed to teach me in secret. The Cultural Revolution was over but it was still dangerous for anyone to teach or practice anything that wasn't sanctioned by Chairman Mao and the communist government. My master taught me some very basic Qigong movements and meditations. He also taught me Kung Fu and Tai Chi.

I really enjoyed this, especially the Qigong. I found that when I did the Qigong part I felt so peaceful. I felt so good about it that whenever I felt miserable I did Qigong. It always made me feel better. I didn't understand why and I wouldn't learn the true power of Qigong for many years to come.

After high school, many of the students like me were sent to live in the country to work as farmers. Chairman Mao said we were being "called upon" to serve our country. We weren't "called." We were forced to go. Soldiers took us.

We were told that we would be "warmly received" by the country people but we weren't. They didn't want us there. This was a poor and lonely, hilly country. People had not enough land to grow food for themselves. Now they were forced to receive one hundred and seventy-five more young people. That meant that they had to give up some of their own land to help us to survive. So we had conflicts. We were given the worst of everything.

Soon, the local government took us to a place that was even worse. The land hadn't been cleared. There was no place to even grow any crops. We worked like slaves, sixteen hours a day, to open up the land for farming. We built our own shelters to live in.

We created the paddies for growing rice but there was no water nearby. So, we carried the water to the paddies in large wooden jars. The closest water was a mile away. When that supply ran low, it was two miles to the next closest water supply. We carried in thousands upon thousands of gallons of water. Still, the land was so poor that no matter how hard we worked we couldn't grow enough food to feed ourselves. Some of the girls became prostitutes in order to survive. If they were caught they were severely punished. Quite a few of the young people nearly starved to death.

In order to survive, I risked my life to catch poisonous snakes to sell in the farmer's market. Poisonous snakes were used to make medicine and they brought a pretty good price. I found that if I could catch three or four snakes a month, I could make enough money to eat.

Whenever the weather was hot, in the early evening, I would take a bamboo stick and sneak off down into the valley near the stream and search for snakes. I took off my pants, tied knots in the legs and used them as a bag to hold the snakes. Then, very early the next morning I would take them to the market to sell.

I would often sneak off at night to be by myself so I could practice my Qigong. Somehow it always made me feel better. It helped keep me going.

The work was very hard and I suffered many injuries and diseases in the country. One time, we were hauling wood, very heavy loads, which we had to carry for miles. There were two of us carrying this huge log down a mountain trail through heavy forest. The log was probably 20 feet long and weighted at least 500 pounds. We carried it on our shoulders with one man carrying the front end and the other the back end. I was the man in front.

The man behind me, just a teenager like myself, stumbled and fell dropping his end of the log. Without any warning, the entire weight of the log came crashing down on my neck, shoulders and back crushing me to the ground. It's amazing that I wasn't killed. My back was so seriously injured I was in bed for two months. From that time on, my back was in constant pain. My feet were in constant pain. I had an infection in my eyes. It was a miserable life.

But, I also learned a lot about traditional Chinese medicine during those years. I learned more about how to use herbal medicine and acupuncture. This was the only kind of medical care the peasant farmers had. It served them well. That and my Qigong and the poisonous snakes I sold for food are what kept me alive.

Returning to Normalcy

AFTER CHAIRMAN MAO DIED and the Gang of Four was purged from power, Deng Tsao-ping became the most powerful man in China. All of the Chinese people are very grateful to him for the positive changes he made. The dark, terrible days of the Cultural Revolution were finally over. Slowly, China started becoming a modern country.

The colleges and universities were reopened. Young people like me were allowed to leave the countryside and return to our homes. I was even allowed to take the very first college entrance exam, which was a miracle in itself. I did well on the exam but didn't get to go to college then. I had no relatives or contacts who could help me. And, I still carried the legacy of being the child of "bad people" and that would continue to haunt me.

A young man, who had been my very good friend, or so I thought, suddenly became very jealous and turned against me. He was very angry that I was allowed to take the college entrance exam and he was not. So, he went to the county government and made false accusations against me and told them I was a bad person. Because of that, despite my exam scores, I was denied the opportunity to start to college.

Once again, I was being harmed because of someone's lies; someone I thought was my devoted friend. We had known each other for many years and had worked side by side in the country. Many times I had come to his aid and always shared what little I had with him whenever he needed it. I could not believe he would do such a thing to me. This only served to increase my anger and distrust of people.

It was not my fault my friend could not go to college. It was the law. He was already married and the government had ruled that married men could not attend college. My friend could not take out his anger and frustration on the government so he took it out on me.

The next year the central government sent out orders that all young people could return to their hometowns and I did. I got to take the college entrance exam again and finally I was allowed to go to college. My life started to improve, at least on the surface.

After all I had been through, I was a very depressed and angry young man. I did not want to talk to anybody. At school I had no true friends, no soul friend. Most of the time I sat alone and did my own reading. While I didn't act like it outwardly, I actually hated people. In fact, I hated everything in the world, though I did not say it. I saw everything in a negative way.

If someone said, "Wow, the flowers are so beautiful." Immediately, in my head, I responded, "Hey, flowers.

Nothing to be proud of. Tomorrow you will be as dead as salted fish!" To me the world was just upside-down. I hated the way the world was. Sometimes I wanted to just leave this world. I was searching hard for an answer to life. Soon, the answers started to come.

During college my interest in Qigong was renewed and expanded. I met a nun who was very knowledgeable about Qigong. I told her I wanted to learn from her everything she knew about Qigong. Before she would agree to teach me she asked me why. Why did I want to learn?

At the time, both of my parents were very sick. I told her I wanted to help them get healed. That's what I wanted most. Secondly, I told her I wanted to help other people. She said no one had ever told her that before. She said most people wanted to learn how to increase the power of their own Qi, to help themselves, or for martial arts, something like that. But, I didn't want to learn martial arts Qigong. I just wanted to help my parents get well.

She was so surprised with what I said she agreed to help me. But, she said her master would not allow her to teach his technique for helping others to heal. She did agree to teach me what she could and I learned from her a technique for enhancing my own Qi. I practiced it diligently. What I still wanted most was to learn how to help others. In time, with the help of masters I didn't even know of yet, I would learn how.

While I was in college I fell in love and married a beautiful young classmate named Fang (pronounced Fahng). After graduation I became a college instructor and within a few years the head of my department. I was dedicated to education and helping to improve the lives of my countrymen through learning. My life was getting better. Lots of good things were happening but I was still very angry deep inside, still very disillusioned.

I was still searching for the meaning of life, for enlightenment. Ironically, it would take another serious injury and even more physical pain before I found the answers I was seeking.

Focusing on Qigong

AFTER MY EXPERIENCE at the soccer field, where my basketball injuries, indeed all my old injuries going back to childhood, were healed so miraculously, I devoted all my free time to Qigong practice. I practiced at least two hours a day, sometimes four or six hours and even longer when I had a day off. I just loved it. I found it was so powerful.

Some people are doubters and there were people like that around me. They said that Qigong was a psychological thing, all in your mind and nothing to get excited about. But, after what I had experienced I knew it was more than that. I practiced and practiced and did research on Qigong.

I felt so happy and joyous inside now. All my hatred was gone. I was not depressed any more. I looked at things in a positive way. That day at the soccer field the Qigong master had talked about the power of forgiveness. Not just saying the words but having true forgiveness in your soul. He talked about how powerful that kind of forgiveness is. How it increases the flow of Qi in your body. He talked about how your body and mind and spirit are all one. He said that without true forgiveness you could never be completely healed.

I knew what he was saying was true. I had suffered so much and I was filled with anger. I had never forgiven anyone or forgotten what they'd done. I was even angry with my parents. I was so little when the nightmares of the Cultural Revolution started I could never understand how they could run away and leave four little children to face so many dangers alone. I loved my parents and respected them but I had never forgiven them. I had never forgiven myself for being so angry either.

I took what the master said to heart. Then, in my meditations I recalled each of the people I knew had hurt me by name and I forgave each one of them by name. I no longer blamed them. I realized now that the former friends who had turned their backs on us had little choice. If they'd helped us they would have suffered the same fate. I forgave them and later on we were able to renew our friendships.

I forgave my parents. I forgave myself. Once I did this, it was like 'snap,' I was free. The very next day I felt completely different. My chest felt so open. When I looked around, everything looked so beautiful. Then, I realized my Qi, my energy, was so full. My soul felt so free. It was so wonderful.

After that, the healing took place so fast. All the pain in my body, all the problems in my back, my feet, my knees, my eyes, were all gone. I felt as if all the pain and problems had just shot out of my body to the end of the universe. They were just gone. Completely gone.

During the first two months of practicing what the master taught us, my entire life changed. For the first time, I had experienced the healing power of Qigong and I knew I wanted to make it a part of my life to help others. But, I didn't know how.

The master did not teach us how to help others to heal. But, during one of my meditations I could see him so clearly and I heard his voice say, "You can use my energy together with your energy and through your visualization you can send this energy out to help others to heal." I knew it had to be true. So, I tried it.

My father-in-law had a very bad stomach problem. He could hardly eat anything at all. So, in my meditation, I visualized myself going into his stomach. I saw lots of junk stuff inside so I took it out. I visualized this window in his stomach and I just kept grabbing this junk stuff and throwing it out the window. Then, I saw these little holes, dark spots, black spots in his stomach and I visualized the energy coming in, gold energy, white color, whatever came to me in my meditation I just used it to smooth out his stomach and soothe it.

Later, when I saw him, I asked him how he was feeling. He said from about three-thirty to five o'clock his stomach just started singing like crazy. He was working in the street, selling clothes at the time. He didn't know what was going on but when he got home that night he was so hungry. He just started eating. He couldn't believe it. His stomach was fine. I just said to myself, "Wow!" And, since then, his stomach has been fine. He was healed.

I also used this technique to help a couple of my students who had asthma and sinus problems. It was during a school break and when they got back to college they told me they had thrown their medicine away. They had each gotten this feeling they didn't need their medicine anymore. So, they threw it away.

I spent as much time as I could practicing the movements and meditations the master had taught us. I practiced his teachings for about a year and a half. Then, something happened to my wife.

My Wife's Tumors

IN 1987, MY WIFE, FANG, went to America to teach as part of the American Field Service program. She was gone for a year. It was not a happy time for her and she returned very depressed. She noticed a lump in her right breast. We went to the hospital and they did an operation and removed the lump and said it was not cancer. We were so relieved, thank God, it was not cancer. They said the operation was very successful.

But, within a few weeks she noticed more lumps. Within two months the doctors found five lumps in the right breast and two in the left. The doctors said they did not know what to do about it. They asked us to wait for a couple of months and see what would happen. Maybe they could afford to wait, but we couldn't. We were ready to try anything.

Despite the success I had had helping others, I did not have the confidence to try this on my wife. The thought of

47

cancer was just too frightening. Then, I heard of another Qigong master who was coming to town. This was Master Yau, who was from the Shaolin temple. Later, I learned he was a colleague of my previous master.

We went to a class he was teaching in a park and after the class we went up to him. I told him my wife had a serious problem and before I could explain anything he said, "I know. She has four lumps in her right breast." Then, he paused a little bit and said "no, no, no, five, five. There's another one, a little one, behind the biggest one. The biggest one's as big as an egg. The smallest like the end of a thumb, hidden behind the biggest one." I said, "Wow, that's right." Then, Master Yau said, "Oh, and then on the left side she has another two."

Because this was such a closely kept secret and he knew exactly what was wrong with her immediately, I knew we could trust him. He said he was able to 'see' inside the body sort of like an x-ray. He was in his sixty's but he looked twenty years younger. We knew we had found another real Qigong master. He agreed to help Fang and I took her to see him every morning at five o'clock for twenty days.

All of the tumors in her left breast were completely gone. On the right side only one tumor was left and it had shrunk down to a very small size. We wanted to thank Master Yau in a special way. So, one afternoon, I bought bananas and we took them to him. There were 13 people with him that day sitting in the room. He said, "Today, I do not have time to do healing for everybody so now I want to do a group healing." I had never heard of a group healing before.

Master Yau took the bananas I had brought and said, "I want each of you to take one of the bananas and hold the banana up. I'm going to pass energy into the bananas. I will use my Qi to cut the bananas and they will be cut into two or three pieces without damaging the skin. And, inside you will see the color change into a purple column from the top all the way down to the bottom." I thought to myself, "this I've got to see."

Master Yau had me give a banana to everyone in the room. We held the bananas up and he raised his hand and made a slight pumping motion. It was amazing for me. I could literally see the light coming out of his hand. After a few seconds, he said he was finished and that the bananas would help with the liver or stomach or whatever problem the person had. He said, "My energy is there now."

So, we pealed open the bananas. Outside, the skins were completely unchanged, not a mark on them. But, inside, every banana had been cut into either two or three pieces just as if someone had sliced them with a sharp knife. And, when we separated the pieces there was a column of purple color running right down the middle just like he'd said.

Like most people, if I hadn't seen it for myself, I wouldn't have believed it. But, I'm the one who brought the bananas and he had no way of knowing we were even coming that day. It was amazing!

Then, he said he wanted to make another demonstration. He grasped a piece of paper from the table, newspaper. He put it in his hand and just stared at it. Within one or two minutes, smoke came out and then, Voom! Fire. I just said, "Wow."

After my first master's meditations, my back pain completely went away but I still had two bone spurs on my spine. So, I asked Master Yau if he could do something for my back. He said, "Oh, yes." He used two fingers to touch my back. Within one or two minutes, his fingers felt like two burning hot iron stakes. Very, very hot. Oh, you just don't know the sensation. It was like fire burning there. Later, when I got home I found two fingerprints on my back where he touched me.

To tell the truth, I also wanted to test Master Yau to see whether the burning paper was real or not. Many people called themselves Qigong masters but they were fakes. They would make demonstrations like that but put some sort of chemical on the paper and hold it in the sun and it would burst into flames. Like a magician's trick. So, I still did not trust him completely. But, after he touched me with his two fingers, and the bone spurs completely disappeared, I totally believed in him and told him I wanted to have him teach me.

He agreed to be my master but told me I could only practice what he taught me and no other Qigong. He stared at me straight in the eyes and the smile that was always on his face disappeared for a moment. He was very serious. I agreed but in my mind I thought this was very selfish. I thought, you're not the only guy in the world who can teach Qigong. I had learned a great deal already but after what I'd seen Master Yau do I knew there was much he could teach me. He had his reasons and eventually I would understand why he taught me this way.

His teaching was very strict. You had to perform the meditations and movements exactly the way he said and at a precise time each day. If you messed up, you had to start all over again. I learned to breathe in a way that was so deep and yet so gentle I couldn't even feel the air moving through my nose when I would inhale and exhale. I learned to use my whole body to breathe and to gather energy.

I studied from Master Yau for about a year. I did exactly what he said to do at the exact time he said. When he told me to go to Ding Hu Mountain to practice, I went. It was a very spiritual place with a famous temple up there. I always did exactly as he said. Then, one day he told me he was leaving. I was stunned. I said, "After you go, what should I do? Who will teach me? How do I get in contact with you? Where can I find you?"

"You don't need to find me," Master Yau said. He told me to keep practicing what he had taught me and when I was ready someone would come to teach me or I would get a message from him in my meditation.

I practiced what he taught me for several more years, always very careful to do exactly as he'd said. Many other Qigong masters came to my town but I did not go to see any of them. Then, one day Master Yau came to me in my meditation. He just appeared as clearly as if he were standing right in front of me. He said, "Now, you are ready to explore whatever you feel is right."

I went to see many different Qigong masters who were giving workshops. Just by attending for ten minutes, I knew what level these masters were and what kind of techniques they were using. I knew whether they had anything to offer me. I was really grateful to Master Yau for his advice. Now, I understood how important it was to stay with one master until you are ready to move on. But, you need to find a master who really knows meditation and who knows the power of Qigong and knows how to explain it to you. If you just wander around trying one thing after another you are just wasting your time. To this day, Master Yau still appears in my meditation from time to time.

My First Trip to America

I N 1992, THE OPPORTUNITY came for me to go to the United States through the American Field Service. I was asked to go to a high school in Minnesota to teach Chinese and Chinese culture for one year. Fang's experience of being in America away from me and our home for a year had not been a good one. So, I had never considered doing this myself.

Besides it was very rare for two people from the same family, a wife and a husband, to be asked to be part of the AFS program. It was a very unusual set of circumstances that led to my being asked to go. Others with similar qualifications to mine had turned down the offer. The college wanted to send someone and I was the most qualified person left. So, they asked me to go.

While I had never before thought about going overseas, just before this opportunity came I got a message in a meditation that I would be going to the United States. It now seemed like something I should do. We decided I should go.

About a year before the offer came for me to go the United States, I got a message from Master Yau that I would soon find a master whose technique was good and it was time for me to study his technique. There are thousands of different types of Qigong exercises. In China, the bookstores are filled with them. But, a couple of things happened that kept bringing me back to one man, Master Zhang. One day I opened a magazine and there was a story about three Qigong masters. One of them was Master Zhang and his picture just jumped out at me. His eyes were like a real person's eyes. They were just sparkling in the picture.

I got his book and his videotape right away. His teaching was unlike anything else I had learned and his movements were very simple compared to the other styles of Qigong. I liked it a lot and began to practice what he taught. It was very powerful.

From all the years I had studied and practiced Qigong, I knew how powerful it could be to help people heal. But, most of the teachings were very complicated and required so much time and dedication to learn. They said it took years before you could learn to use Qigong to heal another person. Some said ten years, others fifteen years. Some said fifty years. Even then, most Qigong masters kept much of what they knew secret and revealed these secrets only to a select few. In fact, some of what I have learned from some of my masters I am not allowed to reveal to anyone.

This never seemed right to me. From the very beginning of my Qigong training a voice kept saying to me, "Qigong is simple. It is so simple. Anyone can do it.

53

Everyone can do it." Master Zhang said similar things in his teaching. Now, I was finally beginning to see how simple Qigong really was and how it should be taught.

After I arrived in Minnesota, some people took me around to see some of the lakes. I had never been to the U.S. and knew nothing about the state of Minnesota. Strangely, the land and the lakes looked so familiar to me. Then, I remembered a meditation I had that showed me a land to the north with lots of lakes, lots of water. In my meditation I traveled to this land from China and now here I was. This was that land.

I taught Chinese and Chinese culture during the day at the high school in Inver Grove Heights and at night I taught Tai Chi. There was a lot of interest in Tai Chi and many people came to my Tai Chi classes.

I became very good friends with another teacher named Dennis Schuler. Dennis taught history and was also the hockey coach. He's also coached football and basketball. He's a very talented man, a good man and very helpful to me.

One day we were talking and I told him that what while I enjoyed Tai Chi what I was really interested in was Qigong. Qigong was really my specialty, I said. He had never heard of it so I told him that Qigong is sort of a Chinese breathing exercise, by controlling your mind and body you can control and balance the energy in the body and help the body to heal. He just looked at me and said, "Oh," and started talking about something else.

Dennis did not find Qigong very interesting until one day I went to Dennis' house after school. He went to change his clothes and while I was waiting in his living room I saw a dog lying over in the corner of the room. I called to the dog and waved at it and clapped my hands and the dog totally ignored me. I called out to Dennis and asked, "What's wrong with your dog?" He said, "She's deaf. She's just old and deaf."

I asked him if it was okay if I worked on his dog and he said, "Sure." He didn't know what I meant. He was just being polite. But, I wanted to help. So, I sent a signal to the dog and got her attention and slowly she got up and came over and laid her head on my lap.

I worked on the dog for about five minutes or so, clearing the blockages in her ears and head and balancing her energy. When Dennis walked into the room, I said, "Dennis, your dog can hear." He looked at me kind of strange and said, "You're kidding?" I said, "No. Try it."

So, Dennis clapped his hands and called, "Tory, Tory, Tory," and right away the dog responded to him. She ran over to him, her tail wagging and started running around his legs like a puppy. Dennis said, "Wow," and just stared at me for the longest time.

Suddenly, Dennis grabbed a chair and sat down and said, "Lin, Lin, (everyone called me Lin) try it on me, try it on me, my knees." Dennis had been a hockey player and a football player and he suffered many injuries in his life. He was always in a lot of pain. His knees were so bad that when he tried to enlist for military service he was rejected because of his knees.

I worked on Dennis' knees for about five minutes or so then I said, "Okay, Dennis, stand up and move around." He got up and started to move, then he jumped up a little, then he jumped up a little higher. He was jumping up and down and he said, "Wow! Ninety-five percent of the pain is gone." He couldn't believe it. "You have to teach this stuff," he said.

The next day after school Dennis took me to the community center and we arranged for me to teach a Qigong class. We wrote up an announcement saying, "Come learn Qigong - Chinese breathing exercise."

When it came time for the first night of class it was held in the school cafeteria and only five people showed up. There we were, just the six of us, sitting around a table in this big, empty cafeteria. I asked everyone why they came and when they told me I just shook my head and thought this is going to be a very interesting class. (The class eventually grew to seven people as two more joined us later that evening.)

Two of the five were there by mistake. They thought they'd signed up for a different class. Another woman had come in wearing an oxygen mask and wheeling this big oxygen tank behind her. She was an older woman named Esther Trejo and she made it very clear that she didn't want to be there.

When I asked why she was taking the class she said it wasn't her idea, it was her son's idea. Her son was a martial arts student. He'd heard about the class and thought it might be good for his mom who was having serious problems with her lungs. Esther thought it was a terrible idea. She told her son, "I don't need some Chinese man coming over here teaching me how to breathe since I've been breathing on my own for 60 years."

But, her son wouldn't take no for an answer. He drove to his mom's house that night, put her in his truck, drove her to the school and left, telling her he would be back when it was over. It was winter time and winter is cold in Minnesota so Esther didn't have much choice but to go inside. As she put it, she was "stuck."

I started the class by saying, "Let me make a demonstration." I asked if anyone had any pain in their wrists or neck or back or shoulders or anywhere. Esther said, "Yes, in my wrist. I have to drag this tank around 24 hours a day and it hurts my wrist." I asked her to put her wrist on the table, close her eyes and relax. I worked on her wrist, taking out the blockage and the pain and after a few minutes I told her to open her eyes and try using her wrist. To her amazement the pain was gone.

Esther kept coming back to class and by the fifth week she walked in still dragging her oxygen tank but she wasn't wearing the mask. She was doing so much better she only needed the oxygen when she exercised. By the eighth week, Esther was off the oxygen completely and has been ever since. You can read more about Esther's story in her own words on page 249 of this book.

When word of Esther's experience got around, a reporter from the St. Paul Pioneer Press newspaper came and did a story about my class and soon more and more students were signing up to learn Qigong. During my stay in the United States that year I was able to use my Qigong techniques to help many people, scores of people, to heal.

This was all further confirmation to me that Qigong was supposed to be my life's work. Qigong was what I enjoyed most. Being able to help people, to help remove their pain and help them to heal, is just the most wonderful thing I could ever hope to do.

My wife and baby son couldn't come with me for my year in Minnesota. As a result, I had a lot of free time and spent hours meditating and practicing Qigong every day. I would start at 10:30 or 11 at night and often meditate until the wee hours of the morning. It was during this year that my life's mission was revealed to me. I was to become a Qigong master myself. I would use my knowledge to create and teach a new style of Qigong. A style that was so simple anyone could learn it.

Many people wanted me to stay in the United States when my year was up. They offered me jobs and whatever I needed. But, I always said no. I wanted to go back to China. I knew it was what I was supposed to do. I also missed my wife and baby son very much. However, I had a very strong message within that I would be returning to the United States one day. I had no idea how this would happen. I didn't have a conscious desire to return to America. I wanted to go home to China but the message was clear, one day, for some reason, I would return.

Becoming a Qigong Master

AFTER RETURNING TO CHINA, I devoted my time to my Qigong meditations and practice. I was now the Dean of the English department at my college and was in charge of making the teaching schedules. I arranged all of my classes into just a couple of days a week giving me as much time as possible for Qigong.

During my years of study I had spent days and weeks at a time in Qigong meditation and practice. Sometimes I spent a month in meditation, sometimes as long as two months.

The first winter after my return home, I took two months off to go to Master Zhang at Qing Cheng Mountain. I spent those two months mostly in deep meditation deep inside a cave. First, there was a three day fast and meditation in the cave. Then, a week-long meditation and finally a month-long meditation. During these meditations I was allowed little or no water and very little food. During the month-long fast and meditation I had just three apples to eat and a few small bottles of water. This was a test of your ability to control your Qi and a test of your discipline.

These deep meditations had always been a key part of my Qigong training. My masters often had a very specific message for me to focus on in my meditations. This training is so enlightening I don't know how to explain it. But, the purpose and the result are always the same; to enhance your understanding of the universe and to increase the power of your own Qi and your ability to focus it.

My training with Master Zhang was more enlightening and beneficial than I can put into words. At the end of this training I was given a series of tests. The master tests you primarily on your ability to read the energy in other people's bodies and then to use your own energy, your own Qi, to help them to heal.

You are also tested on your ability to read people's thoughts. You are tested on being able to predict the future. One test is to predict what the weather will be for the next ten days. If you fail these tests, you do not pass.

There are many other tests as well. Some would be considered very dangerous for anyone who was not a Qigong master. In one test, I was taken into a room with an electrical transformer. There were two electrical lines. One positive, the other negative. They carried 220 volts of electricity. I had to grasp one line in each hand and use my body as a conductor to complete the circuit. It is another way you show your ability to control your own energy. Obviously, I passed the test. But, please, don't try this test yourself. It would be very dangerous and could kill you.

In another test, I had to change the alcohol content of wine. I had to raise the alcohol content in one bottle of wine and lower it in another. All of these tests I had to pass and did pass with very high marks. But, again, most of the tests focus on your ability to use your Qi to help others to heal.

I tell you these things to give you an idea of what it takes to become a Qigong master. It takes years of dedicated study and training.

At the end of my testing at Ching Chang Mountain with Master Zhang I was awarded certification as an International Qigong Master. I had not gone there expecting anything like this. I went only to study with a master for whom I had the greatest admiration and respect. The certification came as a complete surprise. It also came as further confirmation to me that I was on the path I was meant to travel for the rest of my life.

China is a large country and the Chinese people speak many different languages. Some of them are as different as English is from Russian. Because I am fluent in five Chinese languages, I had the good fortune of being able to study with many diverse Qigong masters. Some of these masters I cannot mention by name in this book and some of their teachings I am required to keep secret. My failure to refer to these masters is in keeping with their wishes. I greatly respect all of them for their skill and dedication to helping others.

However, what I learned through my more than two decades of Qigong training, research and practice is that the ability to heal, the ability to use your energy, your Qi, to heal yourself and to help others to heal is something you can learn to do right away. What you will learn in this book will not make you a Qigong master. But, the wonderful fact is that you do not have to be Qigong master in order to awaken your natural healing ability and put it to use.

Like anything else, the more you practice, the better you will become. But, the essence of Qigong is very, very simple and yet incredibly powerful. This message just kept coming to me from the universe that Qigong is so simple. It is what led me to create Spring Forest Qigong.

Part Two

An Introduction To Qigong

"A healer in every family and a world without pain."

An Introduction to Qigong

AFTER READING MY STORY and those of some of my students in this book you might think Qigong is something mysterious or magical or supernatural. Albert Einstein said, "The most beautiful thing we can experience is the mysterious. It is the source of all true art and science."

It is the mystery that leads us to wonder and to search, discover and learn. Once the discovery is made and you reach understanding then the initial mystery is gone.

Qigong is like this. It seems so mysterious to many. But, once you understand it you see that Qigong is not mysterious, just a wonderful gift that is available to everyone.

Hearing music coming out of a radio might seem mysterious or magical or supernatural to someone who's never heard of a radio. You can't see the radio waves. You can't touch them. But, they're real. You don't have to believe a radio will work. You just turn it on, tune it in and it works. If you learn the basics of how a radio works, then there's no mystery at all.

Let me explain the basics of how Qigong works.

You and Qigong

Even if you've never heard the word Qigong before, you've been doing it all your life. You've been practicing a type of Qigong since you were born – sleeping. In fact, you practiced Qigong a lot when you were a baby. Sleeping is a type of Qigong.

Scientists still don't know why we sleep. The heart still functions while we sleep. The blood still flows. The lungs breathe. Your brain is still active. So are your muscles, just ask anyone who tosses and turns a lot. But, physiologically there is no reason for sleep.

So, why do we sleep? Sleeping is a natural meditation. Sleep is one of the ways we're born with to help balance the energy in our bodies. That's why we need sleep. Qigong is all about energy balance. So, you see, sleep is one type of Qigong.

Physical activity is the Yang part of our everyday life. Sleep is the Yin part of everyday life. As in all things, Yin and Yang need to be in good balance.

How do you feel after a good night's sleep? When your energy is well-balanced, you feel great. When you don't have a good night's sleep you don't feel so great. Your energy is out of balance. Sleeping is a passive way of practicing Qigong. By learning more and practicing Qigong in an active way you can learn to maintain that balance. Qigong can help you to sleep better and feel great, rested, relaxed and balanced.

Qigong comes from China. The history of Qigong predates written records. Some archeological studies have found evidence of Qigong practices as far back as 7,000 years ago. Thousands of different styles of Qigong have been developed over the millennia. Some are still steeped in mysticism and secrecy and taught to only a select few.

Today, in China, millions of people practice one style of Qigong or another everyday. You can see them in any park by the hundreds and thousands. They practice Qigong for a very practical reason. They want to feel good and live a healthy, balanced life.

Qigong comes from two words, Qi (pronounced chee) and Gong. Qi is the universal energy that makes up and flows through everything in the universe. In our bodies, Qi means vitality or life force. Gong means to practice, cultivate or refine, leading to mastery. So, Qigong means to cultivate or refine one's vitality or life force through practice.

Qi energy has two basic forms, Yin and Yang. For a person to be in perfect health, Yin and Yang must be in perfect balance. Your body, everyone's body, has two kinds of Qi — internal Qi and external Qi. The Qi moving inside the body to keep the body alive is called internal Qi. The Qi sent out by a healer to help others to heal or do things outside the body is called external Qi.

We are all born with this vital and intelligent energy, Qi. It is comprised of an informational message and its carrier. It is the complex energy substance fundamental to life itself and to all things, animate and inanimate. When Qi flows, life continues and health is obtained. When the flow of Qi pauses or is interrupted, you get sick. When Qi stops, that is the end of life.

So in Chinese medicine and meditation, people always

talk about Qi, Qi, Qi. Moving the Qi or getting the Qi moving is very important in Chinese healing. Qigong is one of the most powerful ways to move the Qi. It works. That's why millions of people do it everyday.

Qigong is all about balance, balancing the energy of mind, body, emotions and spirit. The mind and the body, the emotions and spirit are not separate things. They are all part of you. You can't focus on one and ignore another without causing problems for yourself. Qigong is the simplest and most powerful way I know of to bring about that perfect balance. It is one of the most powerful self-healing practices ever developed. Qigong is truly a health wonder of our world.

Qigong can help you to heal not only physically, but emotionally, mentally and spiritually and all at the same time. Your body, mind, emotions and spirit are all interconnected. In truth, they must all be in balance for you to be completely healed. Through the practice of Qigong you can experience the perfect balance you are meant to have. The benefits of Qigong are as many as there are aspects to life.

Qi (Energy) is Everything

Everything in the universe is energy or Qi. Since the work of Albert Einstein scientists have recognized that everything in the universe, everything we can see and even the things we cannot see, is composed of dynamic relationships of energy. Everything, everything, everything is energy.

A rock, a tree, the air, your body, your mind, all are energy, just in different forms. You are an energy being. So am I. We all are. As Einstein proved, energy can neither be created nor destroyed. But, energy can be transformed, changed, manipulated, put to use.

For example, when you heat water, it becomes steam. The energy of the water still exists just in a different form. That is what the word Qigong means, working with the Qi, the energy, transforming it, putting it to use.

Illness is also a form of energy, but we can transform it into something beautiful and blessing. This is what Qigong healing is about.

Qigong combines meditation, focused concentration, breathing techniques and body movements to activate and cultivate our Qi as it flows through the invisible energy channels, the meridians, of the body. If you're familiar with acupuncture you know it's also based on the energy meridians in the body. But, acupuncture requires a skilled expert to help you. Qigong you can do for yourself.

Qi can flow with the nerve system of our bodies, the circulation system and the meridian system. Qi can also flow on its own without following any systems in the body. This is what makes Qigong even more powerful than any other healing modality.

Understanding Qigong

THE GOAL OF QIGONG is to enhance the quality of your life by teaching you ways to open your energy channels and maintain balance. That is it.

Some Qigong movements are very simple. Others are very complicated and difficult to learn. If you want to learn difficult and complicated movements, techniques and meditations then that is a good choice for you. If you've found a style of Qigong that you enjoy and works for you I encourage you to stay with it. But, in my experience the difficult Qigong techniques are not more effective, just more difficult. I think simple is much better.

In my experience, the best and most powerful Qigong is simple, very simple, yet very powerful. This simple style of Qigong requires less time to learn and to practice while being even more effective and helpful. I will explain more about this in the chapter on Spring Forest Qigong.

THERE ARE FOUR PARTS to balancing your Qi through Qigong: breathing, the postures or movements of your body, your mind & meditation, and the sounds.

Qigong Breathing

Breathing is life. The air we breathe is one of the key ways our bodies bring in Qi. If we stop breathing, we won't live very long. Dogs breathe much faster than people but don't live nearly as long. Sea turtles breathe only a few times a minute and live much longer than we do. Breathing in short, rapid breaths like a dog is not healthy for humans. Slow, deep, relaxed breathing like the sea turtle is very healthy.

Qigong breathing is quite easy to do. You just breathe in slow, deep, relaxed breaths. When you breathe in, pull your lower stomach in a little. When you breathe out, let your stomach out a little. That's it. Just that simple. Yet, very powerful and helpful.

Qigong breathing increases the intake of oxygen and greatly enhances the metabolism of oxygen in the tissues of the body, especially the muscles. Physically, this helps give you more strength and endurance. It also makes you more mentally alert and enhances creativity.

Medical researchers have known for a long time how important proper breathing technique is for a healthy mind and body. This is especially true for athletes or students, and Qigong breathing is one of the most effective breathing techniques. But, Qigong breathing also has additional benefits.

Qigong breathing helps to balance the Qi energy in

your body. The upper part of the body belongs to Yang energy. The lower part of the body belongs to Yin energy. Breathing in is a part of Yin energy. Breathing out is Yang. One of the reasons we get sick is that Yin and Yang energies are not communicating well. By pulling your lower stomach in a little as you inhale and letting it out as you exhale you are enhancing the communication of the Yin and Yang energies. You're taking an active part in balancing your Qi.

If this is not the way you breathe now, just take it slow and easy in learning Qigong breathing. The way you breathe now is not wrong. In Spring Forest Qigong we don't talk about right or wrong; just good, better, and best.

The additional elements to Qigong breathing technique are visualization and focus. As you breathe in imagine you are using your entire body to breathe, see and feel the air, the energy, coming in through every part of your body; now, focus on all the energy you are taking in collecting in your lower energy center, your lower Dantian, which is just behind your navel in the center of your torso.

As you breathe out, visualize any tiredness, pain, sickness or discomfort anywhere in your body changing into smoke and shooting out of your body to the end of the universe. The visualizations and focus greatly enhance the effectiveness of your Qigong breathing.

Now, just try Qigong breathing for a moment. Sit up, take a slow, gentle, deep breath in through your nose and just let your mind relax. Pull your lower stomach in a little as you inhale. Feel the energy coming into your body from every part of your body and focus on it collecting in your lower Dantian (which is behind your navel). Let your lower stomach out a little as you exhale. Feel the flow of Qi through your body in an easy, circular motion.

You're doing Qigong breathing. You're relaxing your mind and body. You're increasing oxygen intake. You're increasing oxygenation of the tissues in your body. And, you're stimulating the automatic, self-healing responses in your body. Congratulations!

My very good friend and student, Patrick, is a psychologist. He searched for many years to find additional methods for helping his patients. Patrick says that if people only learned this simple, relaxed way of breathing, Qigong breathing, they would find enormous positive changes in their mental health. You can read more about Patrick's experiences with Spring Forest Qigong on page 173 of this book.

Qigong Movements

Qigong movements and postures are all designed to help open energy channels in the body and enhance the flow of Qi. When you sit or stand erect you are helping to open the back channel along the spine which is the governing channel in the body. When you open your hand and spread your fingers a little, you are not only opening all the channels in the hand you are also opening the lung channel.

If you have a nose bleed, there is a simple but very effective Qigong posture you can use. If the left side of the nose is bleeding, raise the right hand straight up over your head. If the right side is bleeding, raise the left hand over your head. This simple movement will usually stop a nose bleed in less than a minute, sometimes in just seconds. If the blood is coming out very strongly, you might need to put pressure on the middle finger first by tying a piece of string or something around the tip then raising the hand.

If you look at an acupuncture chart of the energy channels in the body, you'll see that many channels start in the hands and then go to the head and the rest of the body. By raising your opposite arm you are creating an opposing pressure that forces the energy back into the proper channels. Try it. It works.

Raising both arms straight above your head is another simple Qigong movement that helps to open energy channels in your lungs and can help clear your sinuses, help stop coughing and even help with headache. The more severe the problem the longer you will need to hold your arms up to open the energy channels.

These are simple Qigong movements that can be very helpful. However, these movements are treating an immediate need or symptom. The real purpose and great value of Qigong is that it can help to balance all of the energy in your body. Only in this way can we achieve our goal: to enhance the quality of every aspect of your life.

To reach this goal you need to learn and practice Qigong movements and meditations that are designed to balance all of the body's energy at the same time. I will show you a few of these simple, yet very powerful exercises later in this book.

Qigong and the Mind

Some say we use only ten percent of the power of our

minds. Others say only two percent. There is so much we don't know about how powerful the human mind can really be.

A wish, a desire, a thought, your will, imagination, visualization, etc., all come from your mind. They are also all energy and they can be very powerful and helpful to you. Let's play a little game and you can experience what I'm talking about. I call it the Finger Growing Game.

Find the lines at the bottom of your palms where your wrists begin. Put these two lines together then put your palms together. Compare the length of your fingers. Most people have fingers that are slightly longer on one hand.

Now, raise the hand with the shorter fingers and put the hand with longer fingers down and lay it gently on your lower stomach. Slightly stretch open the hand that is up. Put a smile on your face, gently close your eyes and repeat this message in your mind, "My fingers are growing longer, longer, longer, longer... They are growing longer, longer, longer and still longer." Say it to yourself with complete confidence. Just know that the fingers on your raised hand are growing longer, longer, longer. Say it for about 30 seconds to a minute then open your eyes and read on.

Minute up? Okay, compare your hands again. Your shorter fingers became longer, didn't they!

Now, open your hands. Say in your mind just one time, "My fingers come back to normal." You only need to say it once. Line your palms up at the wrists again and compare your fingers now and see what's happened. They've gone back to the same length they were when you started.

Want to play some more? Put the hand with the longer fingers up in the air and place your other hand on your stomach. This time we want the longer fingers to become shorter. Slightly open the hand with longer fingers and say in your mind, "My fingers are becoming shorter, shorter, shorter, shorter..." Focus your mind on those fingers. Feel the energy flowing in the fingers as you say in your mind, "My fingers are becoming shorter, shorter, shorter. My fingers are becoming shorter, shorter, shorter, and even shorter." Again, do this for 30 seconds to a minute.

Find the lines at the end of your palms, put them together and compare your fingers now. Did the longer fingers become shorter?

We don't want to leave them that way, so open your hands and say in your mind, "My fingers go back to normal." Compare your fingers now. They're back to the same length they were when you started.

Isn't this amazing? Congratulations! You've just had your first experience with the power of Qi and Qigong.

Some people have to practice this a bit but most people can do it right away. It's just the power of your mind influencing your Qi. Through your focused thought you sent energy into your fingers causing the finger joints to open or close and the fingers to become longer or shorter. You see, a thought is energy.

Here's a different example. In July of 2002, there was a report in the news about a common knee surgery done for patients who suffer from arthritis. A study at the VA Medical Center in Houston, Texas found that the knee surgery, which is performed hundreds of thousands of times each year to relieve arthritis pain, does not work.

Medical researchers in Texas focused on a group of 180 elderly men. A third had the full surgery, a third had a partial procedure and the remaining third had sham surgery; they were anesthetized and the doctor made three small incisions but performed no surgery. The group that had the sham surgery often reported the best results. In fact, only patients in the sham surgery group were faster walking and climbing up and down stairs than they were before and usually reported the greatest decrease in pain.

The researchers concluded that the third group experienced the "placebo effect." Their improvement was an example of "mind over matter." While some dismiss the experiences of these patients as being "only in their minds," other researchers are beginning to recognize how powerful the human mind can be.

The mind is a powerful healer. Qigong masters and others have realized this for thousands of years. If you learn and practice Spring Forest Qigong you can experience this for yourself.

Qigong Meditation

With the "finger growing game" you've just experienced the power of your conscious mind. What about the other part of your mind, the part that some people call your subconscious and others call your consciousness? It is even more powerful than your conscious mind, much more powerful. It is that part of your mind, your subconscious or consciousness, that you put to use during mediation; but, it doesn't work like your conscious mind. Instead of concentrating hard, in meditation, you let go.

The benefits of meditation have been known for a long time. Meditation relieves stress, which is one of the major causes of disease. Meditation slows the heart rate and respiration. It strengthens the immune system. When you meditate, your brain sends chemical messages to your body to help you relax. Meditation enhances an over all feeling of well-being.

In meditation, the muscles of the body relax. The more completely the muscles relax, the more effective they are accepting and storing oxygen. Qigong meditation not only makes you feel better, it can help make you stronger.

In Qigong meditation, you learn to go into "the emptiness." The emptiness is a place of perfect peace and understanding. The emptiness is a place of perfect quiet and stillness. The emptiness is a place where you can totally renew yourself. The deeper you can go into the emptiness the faster and more completely you can heal your mind and body.

Many people have said to me in my classes that they have done meditation for years but did not get too much benefit from doing it. Some said they have tried to meditate but haven't been able to do it.

It is difficult for some people to quiet their minds. For them I suggest they focus first on the active exercises of Spring Forest Qigong. These movements work like a moving meditation and can help you learn how to get into a meditative state, how to go into the emptiness.

For those who meditate but haven't gotten much benefit I tell them this. You need to let go of everything in your meditation and make a promise to yourself to become the best person you can.

You see, during meditation distractions will come into your mind disrupting your focus - this is your conscious mind at work trying to control your thoughts. You must let go of it. Often pictures or memories from your past will come into your mind. Sometimes these are good memories, sometimes they are bad memories. Either way you need to let go of them. You need to control your mind. This is a simple thing to do. People often make it too hard by trying to concentrate harder instead of relaxing more deeply and letting go.

With good memories, you just say "thank you" to the memory and file it away and return your focus to the emptiness. With bad memories, if they are bad things you have done, you need to forgive yourself, promise to do good things and delete the old memory. Just say "thank you" to the memory, say "it is time for you to leave forever," and clear it from your mind by returning your focus to the emptiness. The past is history. Let go of it. Live in this moment. It is what you do now that is important. This is what you can control and this is what creates your future.

Meditation is a good time for you to purify yourself and your energy. For good things you have done for others, you promise to continue to do these things for the rest of your life. For negative things you have done, you feel true sorrow for doing them, forgive yourself, and promise not to do these kinds of things any more. Then you delete them completely. They are gone forever.

If you still have difficulty releasing these memories or other pictures in your meditation, first bring the focus of your mind to an image that is comforting to you. Think of a place that is beautiful and peaceful and see yourself there. You might picture a beautiful spot by a lake or a stream, by the ocean, or in the mountains, or a beautiful garden. This will help to clear your mind. Then you need to return your mind to the peace, quiet and stillness of the universe - the emptiness.

Meditation is where you utilize both aspects of your

mind to great benefit; both your conscious mind and your infinitely more powerful consciousness. When your conscious mind is filled with all the distractions of daily life it cuts you off from all the wonderful benefits you will receive from your consciousness.

A good way to begin experiencing these benefits is by focusing your conscious mind on one beautiful thing. For example, focus your thoughts on the sun. In your mind, see the sun shining brightly in a perfect blue sky. Feel the wonderful warmth of the sun on your face. Feel the warmth spread throughout your body as you relax more deeply. Focus only on the sun's beautiful rays beaming down on you.

By focusing your conscious mind entirely on one beautiful, healing thought it frees your mind from any distractions, problems or challenges of your life. More importantly it frees your consciousness to take you more deeply into the emptiness.

Remember, Qigong is all about balancing your energy. When your conscious mind is in total control there is no way for your Yin and Yang energies to find balance. The benefits you will receive from this balance are enormous. This alone will take you a long way towards realizing our goal of enhancing every aspect of the quality of your life.

As you learn to go deeper into the emptiness you will find it is a place where you have no fears, no feeling of struggle, no feeling of stress or depression, no pain, no sickness, no anger or jealousy, no feeling of hatred, no wants or desires. The emptiness is a place of perfect peace where you can completely renew yourself.

The active exercises and meditations of Spring Forest Qigong are all designed to help you learn to go into the emptiness and experience its peacefulness and renew yourself.

Qigong and the Sounds

In most Qigong forms, they focus on three key parts to balancing your Qi through Qigong breathing, the postures or movements of the body, and the power of the mind through focus and meditation. Actually, there is a fourth part that is also very helpful and important - the sounds.

Sounds have been used in meditation and balancing the Qi in the body for millennia. In Buddhist meditation, there are so many different chants. For example, the three sound chant "Ong... Ooo... Hong... " Buddhists believe "Ong" to be the fundamental sound of the origin of life in the universe. "Ooo" is believed to be the sound of the beginning of development of life in the universe. "Hong" is believed to be the fundamental sound of hidden power of life development in the universe.

When you chant "Ong", the sound starts from your lower Dantian, which is deep in behind the navel. The energy travels up along the front channel in the body up to the throat and out from the nose. It helps open the front channel.

When you chant "Ooo", the sound starts from the bottom of the throat, goes up to the top of the head, and then comes down to help open all the channels in both arms. You will feel the tingly vibration in the center of your palms.

When you chant "Hong", the sound starts from the chest. It goes up to the bottom of the throat, comes down along the channels in both sides of the torso, until it reaches the bottom of the torso. The energy then goes into the central main channel in the body. After that, the energy will go down along the two legs to the bottom of the feet. This helps all the channels in the legs to open.

Six-Word Chant

"ONG, MA LEE, BAE MAE, HONG"

"ONG" means the heart of wisdom. This is the wisdom of the universe. "MA LEE" means a person's heart, which is full of changes. "BAE MAE" means the purity of the heart, the emptiness. "HONG" means the enlightenment of a person with the wisdom of the universe, or with the power of God.

"ONG" sound can help with problems in the eyes, the ears, nose, and all kinds of headaches and head problems. "MA LEE" can help with problems in the throat, shoulders, elbows, and the heart and lungs. "BAE MAE" can help with problems in the spine, back, kidneys, stomach, and intestines. "HONG" can help heal the problems in the joints of the body and the legs.

In Taoist meditation, there are also many chants. The most popular one is the six-word chant - SHEE, OOO, HOO, XEE, CHUI, YEE. "SHEE" is the sound of spring. It helps with all problems in the liver system. "OOO" is the sound of summer. It helps heal all problems in the heart system. "HOO" is the sound of seasons. It helps with the pancreas. "XEE" is the sound of fall. It helps with problems in the lung system. "CHUI" is the sound of winter. It helps with the problems in the kidney system. "YEE" goes to the THREE-JIAO, which is in the middle section of the torso between the heart and the liver.

As with all things, sounds, too, are energy. And, like all energy, each sound has its own frequency and vibration.

The vibrations of different sounds are well-known and we even have equipment for measuring the vibration and frequency of sound. It is not as well known that the vibration of sound can also help open up the energy channels in the body and help the body heal. Also, for the purpose of meditation, sounds can help you go into the emptiness faster and deeper.

The Sounds of Spring Forest Qigong

In Spring Forest Qigong we practice two sounds: "OHHMM" and "MWAAH." When you chant or meditate on "OHHMM", the energy runs down from the throat to the bottom of the torso along the front channel. When you chant or meditate on "MWAAH", the energy travels up the back channel, called the Governing Channel, along the spine.

These two main channels form the "Small Universe" in the body. Placing your tongue gently against the roof of your mouth connects these two channels. In this way, the energy of the sound helps open the "Small Universe." If we can keep the "Small Universe" open, the Qi will always flow smoothly and remain balanced and there will be no sickness or energy blockages in the body.

(It may be logical to think that people who cannot hear cannot benefit from the use of these sounds. This is not so. People who cannot hear can still benefit from them. Remember, we said that everything is energy with its own vibration and frequency. Thoughts are energy just as sounds are energy. Just focusing the mind, meditating on the words that create these sounds without actually hearing them also makes very good use of the vibration and frequency of these "sounds.")

Each aspect of Spring Forest Qigong, the breathing, the movements, the thoughts and meditations, and the sounds, all work together to help heal the mind, body and spirit completely. You may not be able to see the Qi energy as it flows through your body but it is real and now you have some experience with how the Qi energy works.

Energy Blockages

RIVER OF ENERGY

THINK OF THE ENERGY channels in your body like a stream or river. When the river is flowing smoothly everything is fine. Farmers can take water from the river for their crops. Towns and cities can take water from the river for people to drink. You can even have fun floating on an inner tube down the river on a hot day.

But if something happens to cause a blockage in the river, this can cause a lot of problems. Downstream from the blockage the river can dry up and there is no water to drink or for farmers' crops. Upstream the river can overflow its banks and cause flooding.

With a river it's easy to see that a blockage can cause lots of problems. It is the same with the energy channels in our bodies.

If we want to get well, if we want to feel our best, we have to keep these energy channels open and the energy flowing smoothly and freely. So, when we have blockages, we need to open or remove these blockages to rebalance the Yin-Yang energy.

Everything is energy. You are an energy being. Your mind, your body, your spirit are all energy. While the Qi energy flows through your body life continues. When the Qi stops flowing, this life ends. When the flow of Qi pauses, or is interrupted, you get sick. All sickness in your body, mind or spirit are caused by energy blockages. Remove the blockage and energy balance is restored.

Remember that we are formed by those two kinds of Qi energy —-Yin and Yang. Yin means something female, passive, and spiritual; Yang means something male, active, and physical. Examples of Yin would be woman, water, spiritual life, and earth. Examples of Yang would be man, fire, physical body, and sky. Yin and Yang energies must be in a good balance. Either too much Yin or too much Yang will cause imbalance in the body. We call it sickness. Yin energy cannot live without Yang energy, and Yang energy cannot live without Yin. Also, in a certain situation, Yin energy would change into Yang energy and Yang energy would change into Yin energy.

When Yin and Yang are not in a good balance, a blockage will be formed in the body. Colds, arthritis, depression, tumors, etc, are simply the symptoms of the imbalance of Yin and Yang. This blockage keeps energy from flowing freely in certain energy channels. These energy channels run throughout the body to keep it fully functioning.

We have many energy channels in our body. There are twelve main channels, plus eight reservoir channels. Each channel serves a specific purpose. The main channels carry energy to wherever energy is needed in the body. Extra energy in the main channels flows to the reservoir channels. The body draws on energy in the reservoir channels when the main channels run low.

Blockages in the main channels and reservoir channels prevent energy from getting to parts of the body that need energy. Body functioning slows down or stops, and we feel sick.

Qigong practice lets you remove blockages of the Yin and Yang energies so that the energy can flow through the body in perfect balance. With balance comes healing. With balance comes peak performance. With balance comes inner peace, harmony and happiness.

Qigong exercise and meditation are active and preventative ways to heal the body, while medicine is a passive way to heal the body. Both play an important role, but Qigong can potentially heal the body more effectively and possibly with perfection.

There are many wonderful things that modern medicine can do. I would never recommend that anyone stop seeing their doctor or stop following their doctor's advice. I believe that Qigong can work very effectively with modern medicine as a complementary practice.

I know from experience that people who practice Qigong recover much faster from illness. People who practice Qigong and have chemotherapy for cancer treatment have experienced less nausea, and their hair has grown back much faster. People who practice Qigong and have surgery have experienced less pain and much faster healing.

Modern medicine tends to focus on symptoms and relieving symptoms. While Qigong works much differently focusing on healing the root of the sickness and pre-vention. A perfect healing heals the body physically, mentally, and spiritually at the same time. As far as we know, most traditional healing techniques help the body physically. Qigong opens the door for holistic, perfect healing. This is needed more today than at any other time in the history of mankind.

With the revolution of modern techniques and com-puters, more and more people are working at their homes or in an office. Less and less physical work is required. Because of this, more and more people develop Yin-Yang imbalances in the body. As we have already discussed, Yin energy is something passive. Mental work belongs to Yin energy, while physical work belongs to Yang energy.

Today we use more mental or Yin energy and greatly cut down physical activities, the Yang energy. That means we have created a great imbalance both to our physical body and mental body. Practicing Qigong is the simplest, easiest and best way I know to correct this imbalance in our lives. Qigong is the ideal exercise to help us achieve our goal of perfect health.

When you do Qigong you lead your mind to a state of peace and stillness and you balance the energy in the brain. And, thru the active movements of Qigong you also strengthen the physical energy.

How Blockages are Created

THERE ARE MANY THINGS that can cause energy blockages in the body: accidents, wrong medication, food, even changes in the weather. But, the main cause of energy blockages is emotion. Emotions are good things but unbalanced emotions are very damaging to us.

Stress, Anxiety, Depression

Let me give you an example. To me, stress, anxiety and depression are the same thing, but in different stages. Stress comes first. It can create anxiety and then depression. So, why do we suffer from these things?

Let me share with you a couple of stories.

Past Regrets

Some years ago, I met a psychology professor named Nancy. A Chinese friend had recommended she come to see me. Nancy had been diagnosed with breast cancer. When she came to see me she was severely depressed and completely stressed out.

The first session she did not tell me too much about herself except some medical information from the hospital. She said that the cancer was very aggressive and the doctor wanted to operate right away. She was very scared and did not want to do it. She heard about me and decided to come to see me before making her decision whether to have the operation or not.

I did not say too much about it and asked her to close her eyes and meditate. During the healing, her tears kept coming out. Twenty minutes passed and she said she felt much better. Then she set up five more appointments.

When she came back for the second visit, she told me that her tumor was smaller and she felt very grateful. Each time when I worked on her, she cried. In the fifth visit she said the tumor had gotten much smaller and was now as small as half a penny. She was very happy about that. When we finished the healing, she was so emotional that she started telling me about her life.

She said that she felt so guilty for not taking good care of her husband when he was sick. He died very quickly after becoming ill. It was only after her husband passed away that she realized how much she had loved him. She felt she could not live without him.

She cried everyday and became very depressed. Whenever she was alone, she could not help thinking of her husband. She felt so guilty. She blamed herself and felt she had no hope in her life. Then, one day she found a tumor in her right breast. She was so frightened. She went to the doctor and the tests showed it was cancer.

We chatted quite a bit. At the end of our conversation, I said, "You are a psychologist. I am sure that you know how much our emotions affect our bodies, so let me ask you a question. Everyday you work so hard. For what?" she looked at me and asked back, "What do you think?" I said, "For survival?" "Right," she agreed.

"In order to survive, we do all kinds of things to make sure that our life is protected. We want the best different kinds of insurance we can get. We want the safest place that we can to live in. We want the best vehicle that we can to drive around. If life is for survival, what kind of quality of life are we surviving for, happiness or sadness?" "Happiness, of course," she answered.

"Then, where can we find happiness? Can we find happiness in the grief of the past? Of course, not. No matter how sad you are, the fact is that your husband has already moved on in his circle of life. Your crying and sadness and depression will never help to bring his life back to you. But, it can affect your survival."

"You cannot undo what is already done. If you really think that you owe your husband something, why not you use this as a lesson? In your future, when you have a new friend, you know how to take care of him, or you know how to take good care of your family. You do more good deeds for people around you. Your husband will watch you in heaven. When he sees this, he would be very happy for you and very proud of you too. "

"Throw the heavy sack full of junk stuff on your back away. Look for your happiness today. I think happiness is waiting for you. If you understand what I mean, you don't need to come back to see me. We can cancel the last appointment. Your blockage would go away by itself."

She looked at me and said that she never thought in this way. She said that she would think about what I said. One week later, she came back to see me. She said that she was going to throw the heavy sack on her back away and live a happy life. But she liked to come back to see me because she said that she liked my energy. I have never seen Nancy again.

A couple of years later, a woman came to visit me and said Nancy wanted her to say hi to me. It had been so long I did not remember who Nancy was until she reminded me. When I asked how Nancy was doing she told me that Nancy was doing fine. Her tumor had been gone for over two years, ever since my last appointment with her. She was a very happy and healthy lady now.

Nancy was healthy all her life before her husband died. After that she was so weighted down with guilt it created great stress and depression that contributed to her illness. Those emotions helped cause the energy blockages that in Nancy's case led to cancer. The 'weight' of those emotions caused many blockages in her body that kept her energy from being balanced.

By using Qigong healing techniques I was able to remove the blockages and help restore her energy balance; but, if Nancy had kept carrying that sack of junk stuff on her back, the blockages would have just kept coming back.

Nancy's Blockages

It will probably surprise you to learn that from a Qigong perspective Nancy's breast cancer had more to do with her kidneys than anything else. So, allow me to use

Nancy's case to give you a little more insight into how the energy systems in the body work.

Nancy had blockages in many places. She had some blockages in her heart energy system. These were caused by her feelings but this was not her major concern. Her heart system blockages had not yet affected her physical heart. But those blockages were affecting other energy systems in her body.

Nancy's grief and sadness caused greater blockages and problems with her breathing system or lung energy channels. The strong emotions of grief, because of their specific vibration and frequency, are connected most directly with the breathing system. The blockages in her breathing system, her lung energy channels, were the main cause of Nancy's depression. It is a bit of an over-simplification but Depression is always connected with blockages in this system. Depression is one of the mental problems that can come from blockages in the breathing system and lung channels.

As you might expect, the breathing system includes the lungs, throat, nose and sinuses. But, the breathing system also includes the large intestine, skin and the hair on your skin except for the hair on your head.

A problem in any system can and usually does eventually lead to problems in other energy channels and systems. In Nancy's case, her most serious blockages were in her kidney energy system. This system is extremely important because kidney energy is the life force of the body. Low kidney energy affects all the other systems. Nancy's system was getting weaker and weaker.

Nancy's breast cancer was caused primarily by the blockages in her kidney energy channels. You see, the breasts are part of the kidney energy system. The breasts are physically closer to the heart and lungs but they are not part of the heart energy system or the breathing energy system. The breasts are part of the kidney system as are the bladder, the reproductive organs, the ears and the hair on your head. Nancy's blockages might have resulted in bladder cancer or ovarian cancer as easily as breast cancer.

Focusing solely on the blockages in her kidney channels might well have allowed her body to rid itself of her cancerous breast tumors. But, that would not have solved Nancy's problems. That would have only been treating the symptom and not the overall problem. It would have done little to help Nancy with her depression for example.

Even with those kidney channel blockages removed and the tumor gone from her body, Nancy would have gotten sick again and probably pretty quickly. She might have gotten another tumor in her breast or in another part of her anatomy connected with the kidney system. Or, she might have developed another problem entirely. That would have depended on where the most serious blockages occurred next and which energy channels and system were affected most.

This is why Qigong does not focus on treating symptoms. Treating symptoms is only temporary at best. Remember, the whole purpose of Qigong is to balance all the energy and energy systems in the body. That is the only way we can achieve perfect health and our goal of enhancing the quality of every aspect of our lives.

By removing all the blockages in each of her energy systems, I helped Nancy's body return to balance. But, the blockages would have kept coming back if she hadn't changed her thinking and view of life.

To learn about all the energy systems and channels in

the body and how they interact would require many years of study. The wonderful thing about Qigong is that you don't need to know any of that information to receive the full benefits of Qigong. You don't need to be an automotive engineer to take your family on a lovely drive through the countryside, do you? Of course not, you just need to know how to drive safely.

Learning and practicing Spring Forest Qigong will give you all you need to remove the energy blockages in your body and keep yourself in perfect balance with the energy flowing smoothly. All you have to do is learn and practice.

Future Fears

About the time I met Nancy, a young woman in her twenties named Amy came to see me. She was married and had young children. Her doctor had found lumps in her breasts. She had surgery but another lump developed. There was a history of breast cancer in her family and when another lump was found she was very worried.

When she came to see me it was obvious what was happening to her. I told her that her problems were caused by stress. She worried about so many things. Material things. Financial things. Would there be enough money for things? Would her children get the right education? So much worry. So much stress.

I told her to take things easy. Whatever happens, happens. Whatever doesn't happen, doesn't happen. Don't focus on things. Focus on how wonderful life is. Life is short. You don't have time to worry about all these things. Focus on positive things.

I used the techniques of Spring Forest Qigong to remove the blockages in her body and to help her to balance her energy. After her first visit the tumor was 95-percent gone. It was down to the size of a pea. After her second visit it disappeared completely.

Later, she wrote me a letter. She said that when she left my house after the first visit she just felt so wonderful. She said that she noticed all the beautiful things that were all around her. She said that for the first time in her life she really noticed the birds singing and how wonderful they sounded. She noticed that the grass was green. She said she'd never realized that grass was green before.

So many people go through life not noticing all the beautiful things the world has to offer. A smile. A laugh. A sunset. Or, that the grass is green.

There is nothing wrong with material things. There is nothing wrong in wanting a beautiful house or a fine car or wanting the best things in life for your children. All of these things are fine. But focusing on them, struggling to get them, fearing that you won't have them, all of this causes your energy to be out of balance. It can cause stress and other negative emotions that cause blockages and sooner or latter will result in disease. And, what is disease but dis-ease.

Don't focus on material things at the expense of spiritual things. It's not worth the price you will pay. Keep all things in their proper balance. Please remember, Qigong is all about balance.

Nancy was weighted down by worrying about the past. Amy was weighted down by fears about the future. The result was the same. Their emotions created energy blockages that eventually made them very sick.

By practicing Spring Forest Qigong, you may find, as many students do, all things in your life will start falling into a perfect balance quite naturally and beautifully. As your energy changes and starts coming in to balance, your perception of the things around you, the experiences you have, will also start to change. The way you react and respond to these experiences will also quite naturally start coming into balance. You'll find you are not living in the past or for the future but living fully in this moment. I think you will agree this is the most enjoyable and fulfilling way to live.

The Qi (Energy) of Emotions

CHOOSING HEAVEN OR HELL

LONG, LONG AGO there was a famous military commander who had never lost a single battle. He was the most successful commander in his land. When this commander heard the stories of Buddha, he became very intrigued and wanted to know more of Buddhist teachings.

The commander decided to travel to a Buddhist temple and inside he met an old monk. The commander confronted the old monk with a question and demanded to know the answer. "In Buddhism," the commander said, "there is Heaven and Hell. Where is this Heaven and where is this Hell? Can you show me?"

The old monk asked the commander to sit down and served him some tea. He chatted calmly with the commander about many things but did not answer his

97

question. All of a sudden the monk became enraged. He began shouting at the commander and shaking his finger in the man's face. "You are a monster. You have killed many people. You are evil. You are a devil. Leave this place. Now!"

The commander sprang to his feet in shock and disbelief. Never in his life had anyone dared to speak to him in this way. He was so angry he grasped his sword and yanked it from its scabbard. As he stepped forward to slay the monk, the old man sat back calmly, closed his eyes and with a smile on his face went into his meditation.

This stopped the commander in his tracks. He had never seen anyone react this way to the threat of death. As he stared at the monk his anger went away and he put back his sword.

The monk just sat there and finally the commander turned and walked away. As he reached the entrance to the temple he turned back to the old man and shouted, "You did not answer my question!"

The monk replied, "Yes, I have."

"When?" the commander demanded to know.

"Just now," said the monk. "When you raised your sword to kill me, you were in Hell. When you put it away unused, you came out from Hell and entered Heaven."

The commander stared at the monk for a long while. Then, he put down his sword and seated himself beside the old monk to become his follower. He had become enlightened.

Heaven or Hell? We make that choice all the time. Buddha said, "Where is the beginning? Where is the ending? Everything happening in the world begins because of the heart and ends also because of the heart."

Heaven and Hell are only one door away from each other. If you want to choose hell, you can. If you want to choose heaven, you can. It depends on your wish.

The choices you make are a key part of Qigong. You can choose to be proactive and do things like practice Qigong, or not. You can choose confidence or doubt. To be healed or not to be healed, that is your choice too.

Qi (Energy) Vibration & Frequency

OUR FEELINGS, thoughts and emotions are all energy. Each has its own energy frequency and vibration, as all things do. When that frequency and vibration meets the frequency and vibration of an organ in the body they will produce resonance. When this resonance of "negative" feelings happens too often or is too strong, it can cause damage to the organ. The resonance created by positive, balanced thoughts and emotions can help to strengthen and heal the organ.

This may sound strange to you but there are many eminent scientists who theorize that vibration is key to understanding the universe. It is part of what they call "string theory." Their theory is that the basic building block of everything that exists is not particles but things they liken to an infinitely small piece of "string" with only one dimension. And, it is the *vibration* of the "string" that determines what kind of particles it attracts and therefore what the "string" becomes.

Chinese scholars, in their long time observation, learned that over-excitement affects the heart energy, anger affects the liver energy, fear affects the kidney energy, depression affects the lung energy and too much mental work makes imbalances in the stomach and pancreas energy. If we let these powerful, "negative" emotions stay in the body for too long, the vibration of these feelings will certainly cause blockages, make damage to the organs, and we get sick.

Think of your own life. You respond much differently to a smile than you do to an angry look. A smile is uplifting. It makes you feel better. A smile helps your body relax. Your respiration, heart rate, immune system, every part of you is positively affected. An angry look creates the opposite reaction.

We like the energy vibration from a smile but we don't like the energy vibration from an angry look. The angry vibration hurts the liver energy in your body, while the vibration from a smile will comfort your soul and helps the body to heal.

Everyday in big and little ways we have the opportunity to choose "heaven or hell." We have stress, anger, fear, jealousy, because we choose to have them. They cause energy blockages and damage to the body.

We have many choices. We can choose to ignore these "negative" things when they happen. We can choose to forget them, forgive them, or we can choose to accept them in a positive way. For instance, we can choose to think they are great opportunities to help us grow. And, in reality, that's exactly what they are - great opportunities for us to grow and to purify our own energy.

We have love, kindness, forgiveness, happiness because we choose to have them. They help to heal the body, mind and spirit. The vibration of love energy is the most powerful in healing, whether healing yourself or helping others.

These are not only the most positive choices; they are also the most practical ones. They help you and heal you, while the others hurt you.

I think the choice is an easy one. Practicing Spring Forest Qigong can help lead you to that healthy choice every day. Try it and you'll see. You'll soon find yourself making that healthy choice more and more without even thinking about it.

We are so quick to judge things. Something that seems very negative can turn out to be very positive. When I look at my own life I know how true this is. I went through much pain and suffering in my life that filled me with anger and resentment. Every time something that looked positive happened something else would happen to cause me pain.

But, if it hadn't been for all that pain, the suffering, the injuries, I might never have found my true path. That is the way I choose to look at those things now. Those are the experiences that led me to the greatest joy I could ever have, helping others everyday.

The Qi (Energy) of the Spirit

THE OTHER MAIN REASON we have energy blockages in our bodies is that we lose our spiritual connection. We lose trust in the universe. The energy to heal your body, mind and spirit comes from the universe.

We are from the universe. We live in this body in the universe. And we will go back to the universe, too. Before we have our individual bodies to experience this life, we are one. We all come from the same source, the universe. We come from the universe. We go back to the universe. We are the universe.

Everything in the universe is made up of Yin and Yang energy coming together. These two are always attracted to each other. When the Yin and Yang energies move and encounter each other at a different point in time, a different place in space, and at a different speed, different things are created. That's why there are so many different and wonderful things in the universe. Because they all come from the same source, each one holds all the messages and information of the universe. This is true of everything, including our bodies.

Today, cosmologists and physicists, great scientists, know that everything in the universe came from the same source. Everything we see was created after the "Big Bang", a massive, incomprehensible release of energy. They don't know what form this energy was before the "Big Bang" but they know everything in the universe came from this form of energy.

Our physical body is Yang energy. Our spiritual body is Yin energy. Together they make us what we are. To focus only on our physical body, on physical things, and not focus equally on spiritual things creates an energy imbalance.

Spirituality is not religion, though many religions are very spiritual. Every religion that teaches love, kindness and forgiveness is very helpful in healing and can be very helpful in your practice of Qigong. Without love, kindness and forgiveness your healing cannot be as complete or as lasting.

Remember, thoughts and feelings are energy with different frequency, vibration and resonance. The energy, the frequency, vibration and resonance, of love, kindness and forgiveness are the most powerful for healing.

Qigong is not a religion anymore than the universe is a religion. The universe is simply the universe. The universe is a source of limitless energy that is there for all of us to call upon. In that energy are the answers to all our questions and the source of our healing.

Qigong healing is sometimes called information healing, message healing, signal healing. These are all the same thing just different words. These are all forms of energy. The universe holds all of this energy, these messages, signals, information. And, all of it is available to all of us all of the time.

All the messages of God, Allah, Buddha, Jesus, Lao Tzu are, of course, in the universe. Buddha said that you don't need to go to any place to find your Buddha; Buddha is in your heart. Christ said that you don't need to go to any place to find God; the kingdom of God is living in your heart.

When you trust this information, when you trust the universe, you ask the universe for help, you expect the information from the universe, you are going to get the right kind of energy you need. When this energy joins together with your own energy and you wake up the energy in your body, the power is beyond our imagination.

What is the tool to wake up the inner wisdom and power of the universe in the body? Trust the universe. Surrender yourself to the universe. Forget yourself. The more you trust the universe, the closer you go into the emptiness, the more energy will be awakened in your body.

So, we come to the password.

I am in the universe.
The universe is in my body.
The universe and I are combined together.

Once you say that, relax completely and use your consciousness to FEEL the universe and your body are

105

one. They are merged together such that you cannot distinguish which is your body and which is the body of the universe. The universe and your body are one. Try to stay in this sensation as long as you can. The longer the better. This is the experience of going into the emptiness.

In this way, the frequency and vibration of the energy of the universe, and your body can combine together and stay together longer. The energy of the universe will assimilate that of your body. Then, your energy centers, open, open, open! All the power, the perfect, limitless, healing energy of the universe is open to you to use in your healing!

The exact words you choose to say may be somewhat different. That is okay. The feeling and meaning are the most important. If you are a religious person you may choose to use a religious word to represent the universe. No matter what words you use, if they represent limitless love, kindness, forgiveness and energy to you, that is wonderful, and that is what matters.

The feelings you experience and the pictures you have in your mind will not be exactly the same as someone else. That is okay. We are all different.

Some of my students feel themselves floating through the universe. Others see themselves beside a beautiful mountain lake or by the ocean. One of my students told me she sees herself walking with Jesus.

Just let go of your conscious self and become one with the universe. When you do that, you will begin to experience the emptiness.

As you practice more, your experience and feelings will become ones of perfect peace, quietness and stillness. That is the emptiness. It is very beautiful and very, very powerful. This is where you find the healing power of

Qigong.

Let me share with you a story about another student of mine. He first came to see me for a personal healing and later on he became a Spring Forest Qigong student. When his wife and daughters saw he made such great progress in his health, the whole family became my students. We had so much fun when we met together.

Then, his wife and daughters stopped coming to my class. They had usually all come together but now only the husband was coming. One day, after my class, I asked the husband how his family was. He said everything was fine except Qigong practice.

He told me that one Sunday morning, his wife met someone in their church who told her Qigong was not accepted by God. This person told her God did not ask us to do Qigong. She was told, if we did Qigong, we could not join God in the Heaven after we died.

She was so scared that she stopped coming to finish her Qigong class when she was only half way through. She refused to allow their daughters to attend my class any longer. She also told her husband that if he brought the girls to the class she would divorce him. He did not want a divorce so he came to class alone. He also told me that he strongly believed that some day his wife would go back to Qigong again.

A couple months later, he called to tell me that his wife allowed him to use Qigong on the pain in her shoulders. Soon after that he called to tell me that his wife had decided to allow their daughters to practice Qigong in their rooms.

He said she'd changed her mind because of the positive changes she saw in her husband since he started practicing Spring Forest Qigong. She said he had become more loving and gentle and considerate. She liked these changes a lot and just couldn't see how Qigong could be evil when it led to changes like that in her husband.

Half a year later, he called me one day and was very excited. He said the whole family was coming back to take more of my Qigong classes. Now they've all finished the Fourth Level. They all want to become Spring Forest Qigong healers.

I have also had students tell me that after practicing Spring Forest Qigong they rediscovered their religious faith and started going back to their place of worship. I am always very happy when I hear these stories. I support everything that brings more love, kindness and forgiveness into our lives and our world. It is just so healing, for a person, for a family, for a community, for the whole world.

Again, Qigong is not a religious thing. But, Qigong is a spiritual thing because we are spiritual beings whether we recognize it or not. Love, kindness and forgiveness are very spiritual and very healing. That is why we practice Qigong - to heal. To heal ourselves, each other and our world.

The Qi (Energy) and Peak Performance

AS YOU'VE ALREADY READ, I'm a big basketball fan. I like to play and I like to watch basketball. I don't get the chance to watch much television but I know televised sports are very popular.

Often on these sports programs you hear the coaches or the commentators talking about the energy of the players. They also talk about how the energy level is key to peak performance.

Whenever I hear this I always think the players should be practicing Qigong. Qigong is all about energy, all about peak performance. You simply cannot have peak performance in sports, in health or any other aspect of your life when you have energy blockages in your body and your energy is not balanced and flowing freely the way it was intended to do.

Sports Performance

One of my most advanced and dedicated students was a professional basketball player at one time. At age 20, Jim Nance was recruited to play on a professional team in Europe. Jim had devoted his life to basketball and was looking forward to a career in the NBA after a successful season in Europe. But a series of serious injuries ended his career after just one season.

Jim had suffered back problems for many years. He had done serious damage to both ankles and knees and he suffered shoulder injuries that over time greatly limited his range of motion. "It was impossible for me to keep playing ball," Jim says. "I really couldn't stay on my feet. I'd dribble down the court and all of a sudden I'd lose my leg strength."

Jim had surgery on his back and knee but his medical treatment wasn't completely successful. The sudden end of the career he'd been planning on all his life left Jim suffering not only physical pain but emotional pain which was even worse. "Physical pain I'd lived with my whole life so I was used to physical pain. But at that time I had no direction and it took me years to figure out that my problem was a lack of direction and it wasn't so much vocational as it was spiritual."

For the next 25 years, Jim traveled all over America and around the world searching for answers to his physical and emotional challenges. In 1995, shortly after I had returned to Minnesota he learned about me and came to see me. "In just that first session 80-percent of my pain was gone. I could really move my ankles again," Jim says. "I could move my shoulders. I had full range of motion again and I hadn't been able to raise my shoulders or raise my arms above my shoulders in years."

"What I experienced with Chunyi was so immediate, an immediate kind of release and relief. I felt like a load had been lifted off my shoulders and physically I felt like I could move again without a lot of discomfort and that really piqued my interest."

"Had I known about Chunyi and Spring Forest Qigong back when I was playing I'm sure it would have lengthened my time in sports. It certainly would have helped me physically. Also, it would have helped me with concentration. It would have helped with my attitude. It would have helped with my whole take on how you compete, healthy competition as opposed to unhealthy competition. It definitely would have changed my lifestyle away from basketball. It would have increased my understanding of how certain activities really deplete your energy and others build your energy and strengthen your body. So, I know that I would have played longer."

Based on his experiences Jim believes Spring Forest Qigong would be helpful to professional athletes on many levels.

Jim explains it like this:

Knowledge and Responsibility

"There are athletes and coaches who already are interested in alternative approaches to thought. They're interested in Eastern thought and they do meditation and they do Tai Chi. They don't know this though. It's not the same. The results come quicker with Spring Forest Qigong because you can target specific organs, because you can target specific muscle groups and because you can heal quickly.

It's very different than other forms of healing that I

know of. And you can do it yourself, that's the key.

Many teams might have an acupuncturist, they might have a shiatsu specialist, and many trainers know about acupuncture and shiatsu, and other techniques. However, the athletes don't have the time to study all this so they go to the trainer and say fix me.

With Qigong when they have a pain they can do something about it before they ever have to deal with a trainer or a physician. They can do something right away and then they can go and check with a trainer or a physician to see if something more needs to be done. The difference in this is it makes the athlete more responsible for his or her own health.

When people feel like they can be responsible and they have a payoff that accompanies being responsible, their level of commitment to themselves just goes up. They feel like, 'Okay, I can do this.' They feel more capable. The confidence level increases and that affects performance on the court and that affects life choices off the court or wherever the athlete's involved."

Confidence and Calm

"Just to know how the body works from a different perspective, from an energetic perspective, just helps people have a better understanding of what's going on when they have blockages in the body. And then to know how to remove those blockages, ohh, it's just tremendous what it does for the confidence level. It's so empowering.

There is a sense of well-being and an increased sense of calm they will take into their sport as a result of the work they would be doing with Spring Forest Qigong. In the calm, you don't have the fatigue because the stress level goes down. You don't feel the stress level the same. So, in your body, you don't feel the fatigue the way you used to feel it.

There's a pre-Qigong experience of fatigue and a post Qigong experience of fatigue and they are very different.

If you work with Spring Forest Qigong enough you learn that fatigue is caused by blockages and you can break up those blockages as you're performing and in doing so you prevent the fatigue from taking hold."

Perspective and Values

"It really helps with perspective, with values. It helps you identify what's important in your life. It helps with that process. You begin to realize that you're a spiritual being and it helps you to form a kind of personal relationship with something bigger than yourself. I think without a doubt that is the most important aspect of this. It helps bring a sense of peace and clarity to whatever you do.

There are a lot of athletes who compete and compare and deny themselves all the time. Their whole thing is to be better than the other guy and in the process they lose track of themselves because they are constantly comparing what they have with what someone else is doing.

Qigong opens you up to listening to your internal voices so creativity comes from within as opposed to mimicking something else or someone else.

I think that an athlete today would really benefit from this involvement with Spring Forest Qigong. It makes you a better person first and it makes you a better athlete second."

– *Jim Nance*

If Spring Forest Qigong can help you to be the best athlete you can be that is a wonderful thing, but if it can help you, as Jim says, to be the best person you can be, to live your life with peace, clarity and joy, that is the most important.

Helping Others Perform

Let me share with you another story one of my students told me about an experience she had. My student was watching her son play a little league baseball game when another mother arrived who was limping. This woman was very athletic and had been a competitive athlete in college. That day she was wearing tennis clothes.

My student asked her friend what was wrong. The woman said she'd been running and twisted her ankle. She was really "bummed" because she was supposed to play a tennis match that afternoon and was going to have to cancel it.

My student told her she could help. She told her friend a little about Spring Forest Qigong and the woman asked what she needed to do. My student told her just to put her tongue gently against the roof of her mouth, close her eyes, put a smile on her face and take three slow, deep breaths through her nose. Then, she told her friend to say once in her mind, "My pain is gone. I'm completely healed." Then, she said, just relax and think of something really beautiful, something that makes you happy.

Her friend followed the instructions and my student used the simple techniques she learned in my classes to help her friend. Using these techniques, she helped remove the energy blockage the injury had caused around her friend's ankle. Then, she used these simple

114

techniques to help balance all the energy in her friend's body and help the energy to flow freely.

Within about ten or fifteen minutes, she was done and told her friend to take three deep, relaxed breaths through her nose and then slowly open her eyes. My student was smiling when her friend opened her eyes and said, "Feel better now."

Her friend moved her ankle around a little and then stood up and took a few steps. Her eyes got as big as saucers and she smiled a big smile and said, "I can't believe it. It doesn't hurt. It feels perfect." She was very happy.

My student said her friend called her that night very excited. Her friend said she'd felt so wonderful and relaxed the rest of the day and played one of the best game of tennis she'd played in years. She was amazed.

My student just smiled and started answering all of her friend's many questions about Qigong. Later on, her friend became a student too.

This is a very simple and beautiful story. I hear many stories like it from my students all the time. You see how easy it is to use Qigong to help others. It also shows how quickly things can change and that when you are relaxed and your energy is balanced and flowing smoothly that's when you can achieve peak performance.

Practicing Qigong alone will not make you a better tennis player or basketball player but it can help you to be the best you can be. Whether it is sports or business, your studies, your health, your attitude or your daily life, wherever you seek peak performance in your life, Spring Forest Qigong can help.

Learning Performance

In China they have conducted the most research on the use of Qigong in education. These studies have shown that Qigong does help increase mental acuity, memory and learning ability significantly. In one study among fourth grade students test scores increased an average of 10-percent in just six months.

The students were taught Qigong breathing and a simple Qigong meditation which they did for two minutes at the start of each class. The subjects studied were Chinese language, mathematics and geography. In the non-Qigong group test scores remained about the same at about 82-percent accuracy in these subjects. In the Qigong group test scores went from an average 83-percecnt to 93-percent.

Because education is so important I am currently working with one of my most advanced students who is an experienced teacher to develop a specific program for school children.

Work Performance

Let me share another story with you about how practicing Qigong has helped one of my students in her work. Her name is Marliss. Marliss first came to my classes because she had several health problems. Right away she noticed an immediate improvement in her health.

Marliss says she was always in a lot of pain before Qigong and was never a calm or relaxed person. She always felt "uptight," as she puts it. This was starting to change, as well.

Marliss continued practicing Spring Forest Qigong and

took my Level II class and learned how to use the energy to help others. She says the people at work started noticing the positive changes in her and started asking her what she was doing. When she told them about Spring Forest Qigong, her co-workers started coming to her for help with aches and pains and different things. Marliss says she was so surprised that when she used the techniques she learned in Level II they actually worked. People felt better.

Then, Marliss was given a big and important new assignment at her work. This is how Marliss tells that part of her story and how it helped her to achieve peak performance in her job.

Marliss' Story

"I was the only woman managing basically all men in a manufacturing area. Being the only female working with 48 other male supervisors, the job was very stressful and challenging.

I was asked by upper management to train every employee in the manufacturing area on working with a new labor reporting system. This would accommodate around 700 employees. What that meant to me was that all of a sudden all these factory worker guys would have to learn how to use the computer in order to report their labor. This, to me, was a really big challenge.

In fact, when they gave me the assignment I was petrified. I knew that unless I was calm, collected and focused I wouldn't be able to handle all the pressure and perform at the high level needed to succeed. What I did was put into practice what I'd learned from Qigong and boy did it ever work.

I know without Spring Forest Qigong I would never have been able to accept that challenge, but with practicing Qigong, especially the meditations, I just kind of flowed right through putting together all the training materials and training all 700 workers in the 3 plants.

When I started to train, the employees would ask me, 'Why do we have to do this? How can we do this? Why do we have to change the way we do it now? We never used a computer before.' There was a lot of rebellion (sic) from the employees to change.

I was just able to not let it unsettle me or break my focus. You know, my insides were so peaceful and there were many comments about how calm I looked and how relaxed I was. This helped me with the employees also. Comments from upper management were, 'You just get up there and it's just like nothing, you just train with ease. The employees are afraid when they come to your classes but you are able to have them relax and get over their fear. You get right behind them and show them how to use the mouse, and they're just at ease. By the time they leave they are comfortable and know how to use the computer.'

That was true even when the president of the company came into one of my classes. It was seven o'clock in the morning and the president came to learn the system. The superintendent asked me if I was going to be nervous. I said 'No', because I had done my meditation in the morning. I always made sure that I did my Qigong meditation before I went to teach a class. I would schedule my own classes and I left time for Qigong because I knew I needed Qigong to get through the day. It helped relieve the stress. I know for sure that if I didn't practice Spring Forest Qigong I would have been a nervous wreck up there hyperventilating, etc., because that's a lot of responsibility. Thinking about it now, I know I probably would have never gotten through it unless I did practice Qigong.

It was a great accomplishment for me to be able to put together all the training materials and do all the training for all three plants (700+ employees). I feel confident that all the manufacturing guys were able to go to a computer that they'd never touched in their whole life and report their labor without any hitches. Everything went really smoothly and I attribute a lot of that to Qigong.

I'm not sure how to describe it, the calmness and confidence inside, but I know that it projects on the outside. I never had that before Spring Forest Qigong. I am so thankful for Master Lin and Qigong.

I highly recommend it to anyone who is facing big challenges on the job, especially if they're going to be embarking on something new. It really gives you that clarity of focus and thought you need to perform at your best."

– Marliss Sorlien

I have heard many, many stories like Marliss' from my students. They come to Spring Forest Qigong for one reason and then find it helps them in so many other parts of their life as well.

Qigong is simply the best way I know to balance the energy in your body and keep it flowing freely and smoothly. When your mind and body are calm and relaxed they simply function better. With that you can have peak performance, be the best you can be, at whatever you choose, and enjoy your life to it's fullest. Try it for yourself and you'll see.

The Qi (Energy) and Your Sixth Sense

L IKE THE ABILITY TO HELP heal yourself and others, your sixth sense, your intuition, is something you were born with. While it is an innate ability, over time most of us "learn" not to trust our sixth sense, our intuition. While we may learn to ignore it, it never goes away.

It is that feeling you get sometimes in the pit of your stomach or on the back of your neck or surface of your skin. That feeling that makes you more alert. Or, that little voice that speaks to you quietly, trying to get your attention. That voice that gets drowned out in all the "noise" and activity of daily life. Especially, as we get older.

You may have had this experience, many people have. The phone rings and you know who it is before you answer it. You pick up the phone and sure enough it's that person. Or, someone comes into your mind, someone you may not have seen in awhile, and suddenly this person shows up. Or, you're driving along and suddenly you get a message to change lanes or take a different route and in doing so you avoid an accident.

This happened recently to one of my students. She told this story in the Level I class. It happened to her during the third week of class. She was driving one morning on the highway, in the snow, and all of a sudden she heard this voice from out of nowhere telling her to turn her wheel to the right and get on the shoulder right now!

Without thinking or knowing why, she turned the wheel and pulled onto the shoulder. She was half on the shoulder and half on the highway when suddenly a car came zooming up from behind, out of nowhere, zig-zagging in and out between cars in the snow. It just barely missed her car by inches. If she hadn't pulled over right when she did, the car would have smashed into her at a very high speed.

Much to her surprise she reacted very calmly. Instead of getting mad at the crazy driver for almost killing her, she made a prayer for this young man and then just calmly pulled back on the road and went on her way. Her sixth sense had just saved her from a very serious and maybe fatal accident.

We were born with intuition, with this sixth sense, for a good reason. To ignore it would be like ignoring our sense of touch or taste or hearing or sight. Our intuition can be invaluable in helping us to make good decisions, making us aware of things that we would not even recognize with just our conscious mind or other senses.

One of the benefits of practicing Qigong is that you will

121

develop your sixth sense more. It will help you to make better decisions in your work or at school. It will help you to make fewer "mistakes" in your life because when you learn to hear your inner voice clearly and calmly you will know what you should do and what you should not do.

Practicing Qigong will heighten your intuition and your sensitivity to it. The more you practice and the more good deeds you do for others, the more your sixth sense will develop. You will also develop a very strong protection aura around you wherever you go and whatever you do for good reasons you are protected. "Negative energy" just can't come close to you.

Your sixth sense can come in very handy in many situations. My students have told me many stories about how their intuition has been increased by their practice of Spring Forest Qigong, in many little ways and in big ways.

Let me tell you one story from my own life that came when I was in my late teens and while my understanding and practice of Qigong was still very rudimentary.

After my high school and my time working in the country, I very much wanted to continue my education and go to college. Colleges had only recently been opened again in China and I was very excited about this. However, it was made clear to me that my chances of being accepted at a college were pretty much nonexistent.

I was still carrying around the label of having been a "devil kid" from a "bad family." Also, I had no contacts. I had no pull. There was no one I could turn to in the government. No one in a position of influence or authority who would be willing to take the risk of helping someone like me.

For several months, some close friends of mine and I

122

had been planning to take a very special bicycle trip. It would be what you'd call a vacation. Something I'd never done before in my life.

About a week before we were to leave, I started getting this message from my intuition, my sixth sense. It was subtle at first and kept getting stronger. The message was very clear from the beginning that I should not go on the bicycle trip. I was very excited about the trip, so I kept pushing the message out of my mind.

But, the message wouldn't go away and just a couple of days before we were to leave the message became very strong and very clear, "Don't go on the trip. Don't leave town. Something very important is going to happen." That was the message and it was unmistakable.

I wasn't expecting anything to happen. I couldn't imagine what it could be. But, I finally decided I was getting the message for a very important reason, whatever it might be. So, I told my friends they would have to go without me. They couldn't understand my decision. They were very disappointed and so was I.

The day they left I started getting excited about the message, looking forward to what would happen. But, nothing happened. Nothing happened the next day either, or the next, or the next, or the next. At the end of the week, still nothing had happened. The next day my friends would be returning. It seemed I'd missed the vacation for nothing.

Then, at 9 o'clock that night, a man came to see me. I had met the man before but did not know him well. He wanted to know if I was still interested in going to college. He said if I was that I had a chance. He told me there was a college entrance test being given in a nearby town the next morning. There was one opening left to take the test. If I left that night, I could be there in time.

I left right away and I did get to take the test. I scored very high on the test but I wasn't accepted to college that year. However, the opportunity to take the test that day opened the door for me and two years later I got to go to college.

If I'd gone on the bicycle trip, I would have missed the opportunity. If I'd ignored my intuition, the message from my sixth sense, I probably never would have even known about the test or that I had a chance to take it. Intuition can be very helpful.

As I've learned more about Qigong and become more experienced at it, I've learned to totally trust my intuition and to be quietly aware of it at all times. It has helped me in so many, many ways, everyday. It can do the same for you.

Your intuition is always there, if you know how to hear it. Practicing Qigong sharpens your sixth sense by helping you to become quietly aware enough to hear the messages. Just one more of the many ways Qigong helps you.

The Qi (Energy) of Love, Kindness & Forgiveness

WHILE TECHNIQUE IS IMPORTANT in doing Qigong, what is more important is the way you feel about yourself and the world around you. In fact, the three most important elements in experiencing your perfect and complete healing through Qigong are living a life based on love, kindness and forgiveness.

Love

Love is the most powerful and beautiful of all emotions. Love is one of the most powerful forces in the universe. Our thoughts and expressions of love vibrate at a frequency that is the most powerful for healing, for healing ourselves and for helping others to heal. The vibration of love is soothing, comforting, strengthening and empowering. Love is healing. It is that simple.

This kind of healing love has nothing to do with passion. It has nothing to do with desire. It is not about taking or receiving. It is all about giving. This kind of healing love is true love. True love is absolutely selfless. True love is gentle. It is pure, unconditional, universal love. True love seeks only what is best, making no judgments about what best might be or might not be. To be a true healer, you need to have true love in your heart and soul.

Once you have this true love in your heart and soul, every cell in your body will begin to vibrate with and radiate this healing energy. This loving energy is the only kind you can send out to help others because it is the only kind that vibrates at the right frequency. The greater this love is within you, the greater the healing power of the vibration will be.

True love can bring you wonderful experiences and understanding that you would never have even imagined without it. The most powerful healers are the ones with the purest and most unconditional love in their hearts and souls. The level of healing power depends on the level of love and confidence.

We are all human beings which means we are not perfect. For a human being, true love may seem like an unreachable goal. It might be helpful to think of true love as the sun glistening off the peak of a tall, beautiful mountain.

We may never reach the mountaintop but as long as we are focused on it and moving towards it we are getting closer and closer all the time. And the closer we get the clearer we can see it and more fully we can appreciate it.

Set yourself as a model of love for others. This kind of

benevolent, true love can heal the wound in a human heart in a way no medicine ever could. It is the best medicine for fears, jealousy, sadness, anger, anxiety and so many negative, damaging emotions.

With love, you give yourself a peaceful environment to do Qigong to heal yourself and to help others. What you send out will come back to you. So, when you love others, others will love you, too. Just imagine how wonderfully powerful the energy of that much love will be.

The success rate of my healing for heart problems is very high. I believe the reason is that I really love people. Whenever I do healing for others I take it as a great opportunity for me to share the universal energy with them. I feel very honored to be asked to help them. I look at them as my brothers, sisters, parents, grandparents or children. I consider their suffering as my own suffering.

The heart is the house of the soul and the soul can pick-up on other people's energy. If you really love others, their soul will pick-up on this and open the door for your energy to help them heal.

The great Indian man of peace Mahatma Gandhi described love in this way, "Love is the strongest force the world possesses and yet it is the humblest imaginable." Through the power of love Gandhi helped to change the world. Love is indeed humble and yet it is more powerful than we can even imagine.

Kindness

Let me share with you a story.

Many years ago there was a boy who was always getting in trouble at school for pulling pranks on the other students. He was a very intelligent boy and often used his intelligence to belittle the other students and make fun of them. One day, he so humiliated a girl who was making a presentation in class that he brought her to tears.

That night when his father got home from work and heard what had happened he called his son into his study. Before his father could say anything the son said, "I didn't hurt anybody. I just told the truth. It's not my fault she's stupid. I didn't do anything wrong."

His father had talked with his son many times about his behavior and had a plan he hoped would finally get his point across. The father, who was a big man got up from his chair and picked up a board he had behind his desk.

The board was dark, heavy wood and very highly polished. He handed it to his son and said, "Look at the board and tell me what you see."

The son replied, "A board." What else, the father asked. The son looked again and said, "I can see my reflection."

"Good," the father replied. "I want you to take this board and every time you do or say anything that is hurtful or harmful to another person I want you to drive a nail into the board. And, every time you stop and think and keep yourself from doing those things, take a nail out. You can put in the first nail for what you did today. When all the nails are gone we'll talk again. Until then, I'm taking away all your privileges. You're grounded."

The boy was not happy but he knew his father meant what he said. So he went to his room and drove the first nail into the board. As the days passed, more nails went into the board, some came out and others went it, but finally all the nails were gone.

The son was very happy that night when he went to show the board to his father. The father looked carefully at the shiny piece of wood and ran his hand over the pock marks where the nails had been. Then, he handed the board back to his son and said, "That's very good son, very good. Now, look at what you left behind."

The son stared at all the holes in the piece of wood that once had clearly reflected his own face. He understood now the point his father was trying to make. Slowly, he turned to his father and said, "What do I do about all the holes I've made?"

The father replied, "Be kind."

Whenever we do things that are harmful or hurtful to others it causes damage, not only to them, but to ourselves. Kindness is how we repair the damage, how we fill in the holes.

Love does not have a physical form, whenever you are kind to others you create a stage for love to be presented. Whenever you are thoughtful and helpful and understanding to others, whenever you are kind to another person, they can see your love. They can feel it. Kindness is love revealed.

A true Qigong person shows kindness to all living things. Kindness becomes second nature and happens quite naturally. When you are kind you build up a reservoir of healing energy.

Kindness sends good, healthy messages creating a good, healthy environment for your body and soul. Living in this healthy environment if you do get sick you can heal yourself more easily; when you do Qigong and meditation you can go into the emptiness faster and make a deeper connection to the universal healing energy; and you can more easily let go your worry, your burdens, your fears, your stress. So let yourself be in a state of kindness all the time and feel your spiritual channels open. Then, you will always feel happy in your heart.

Forgiveness

When I first arrived in the America, I was so impressed with the wealth of this country. The parks were so beautiful. The streets were so clean. Everybody enjoyed the freedom of life. Cars were everywhere. Schools were so nicely equipped with modern techniques. Most people had no fear of lack of food. With money you could buy whatever you wanted. In China we did not have these. I was so happy to get a chance to come this country to experience the modern civilization of the world.

But when I stayed here for a few months, I felt that something is missing in this country though I did not know what it was. It seemed that so many people who had so much lived in such fear, fear of losing their job, fear of losing their property, fear of being cheated, fear of being sued, fear of meeting strangers, so much fear.

I also noticed that not many people trusted each other. In business, people did not trust each other. Everything must be documented. Even in families people did not trust each other. So much divorce. So many children living with only one parent. And, while there was much talking, people talked at each other but not with each other. They talked but did not listen. Mostly, nobody listened to nobody.

After a few years, it came to me what was missing in this country. The missing part is forgiveness.

To forgive is of beauty. To forgive is like beautiful art. Fine art opens up our hearts in ways we cannot explain in words. Its beauty touches us in ways we could never experience by consciously trying. Forgiveness does the same.

Forgiveness opens us up and transforms us in ways we could never imagine and we can only know its truth by doing it. We need to have this beauty and this art in our lives, in all our lives. So many things can be settled through forgiveness. Sometimes just by shaking hands. What does it matter who puts his or her hand out first?

When conflicts occur, find a peaceful way to deal with it. Take the fear and hurt feeling away. As a healer, if we do not have this forgiving energy, we will never be able to help ourselves or others to heal the soul.

When someone does something not very nice to you, forgive that person. When you forgive others, you give your love to them. And you give yourself a chance to grow. You give your friend a chance to grow too.

Love is created through forgiving. The more forgiveness you give to others, the more forgiveness will return to you. Then more love will grow within you, within the other person too and within our world. This is the environment we were meant to live in.

And, remember to forgive yourself. This is also important. We are human beings and we make mistakes. When you do something you wish you hadn't done, forgive yourself. Then make yourself a promise to try to do better.

Someone asked me once if someone killed, should we forgive them? If someone started a war, should we forgive them? My answer is yes. Of course, we should.

To forgive doesn't mean to give up. It does not mean we surrender. It doesn't mean we allow them to kill more people. They must be stopped, of course. But how do we stop them, with anger and hatred in our hearts? To this I say, no.

If someone breaks the law they will pay a price for that whether the law catches up with them or not. You may have heard the expression, "What goes around, comes around." This is true.

When you do good things for others, good things will return back to you. When you are loving, kind and forgiving, you will receive love, kindness and forgiveness in even greater measure. Perhaps not from the same people, but it will always come back to you; always.

If you do bad things to others, bad things will happen to you. Sooner or later it will happen. This is the principle of the universe.

I hear people talking about hating people in other political parties or government leaders whose views they disagree with. I hear people talking about hating leaders in other countries who are doing terrible, evil things. Hate the bad things they do, work hard to stop them if you are led to do so, but do not hate them. Hating them hurts you. It blocks the love energy in your heart. Hold them in your heart. This will help them to change much better than your hatred and it will make you a more loving person.

Sometimes people try to forgive through their emotions and find they cannot do it. If this happens, if you can't get past your anger or hurt, then begin by thinking of all the people you do love, all the things you love about this life, and let your heart feel all the goodness in the world.

Then, imagine those you cannot forgive in the midst of all that goodness and the perfect loving energy of the universe. Use the love of the universe to help you. This is a very good way to work on forgiveness.

If you need an example to follow, I cannot think of a better one than Mahatma Gandhi. He devoted his life to the struggle for freedom for oppressed people, first in South Africa and then for most of his life in his native India. Gandhi was a deeply religious man but when asked about his religion he replied, "I am a Christian. I am a Muslim. I am a Hindu. I am a Jew. All men are my brothers."

During his life-long struggle for the rights of others he was repeatedly threatened, savagely beaten and often imprisoned by those in power who opposed his efforts. Yet he never responded with anger or hatred and never called for retribution. He was a man of action but always a man of forgiveness and non-violence.

He accomplished these things through what he called his "soul-force." As Gandhi put it, "It is not that I am incapable of anger, for instance, but I succeed on almost all occasions to keep my feelings under control.

Whatever may be the result, there is always in me a conscious struggle for following the law of non-violence deliberately and ceaselessly. Such a struggle leaves one stronger for it. The more I work at this law, the more I feel the delight in my life, the delight in the scheme of the universe. It gives me a peace and a meaning of the mysteries of nature that I have no power to describe."

Through the power of love and forgiveness, the "soul-force" as he called it, Gandhi led an entire country to freedom. Through this same limitless power of love and forgiveness you too may experience this same peace and discover a meaning of the mysteries of life that are beyond description.

Through this power of forgiveness you will also open

an opportunity for yourself in the future. Let me share with you such a story about forgiveness that comes from ancient China.

Long, long ago, there was a king who held a great feast in the palace for his army commanders. The feast was a big celebration with much food and wine. There was much drinking and some of the king's guests drank too much.

The king had a beautiful wife and she was there. In the middle of the dinner, a great gust of wind came and blew out all the lights. Before they could be re-lit, the queen screamed that someone had pulled her skirt.

A servant rushed forward and lit a candle for the queen. She approached her husband with an angry look and told him someone had touched her skirt in the darkness. She did not catch him but she had grasped the tassel from his helmet. All of the king's commanders wore such tassels on their helmets. Touching the queen was a serious offense and the queen demanded the guilty person be executed immediately.

The king took the tassel from the queen, blew out the candle and ordered that none of the candles be re-lighted. The king threw the tassel into the center of the room and ordered all of his commanders to rip the tassels from their helmets and throw their tassels and helmets into the center of the room also.

Only when this had been done did the king order the candles lit. When light filled the hall again it revealed a great pile of helmets and tassels making it impossible to tell who the guilty party might have been. The commanders must have thought this was some kind of game or joke. Since no one else had heard the queen's complaint to her husband they had no idea why the king had given such an order.

Many months later, the king's land was attacked by an invading army. The king's army was not prepared for the sudden invasion. During the battle to save his land, the king was knocked from his horse. His army was in total disarray and the king had to run for his life as the attackers chased after him.

Suddenly, one of the king's generals appeared by his side. He fought valiantly to save his king. The general thwarted attack after attack all by himself. The general's courage inspired the other commanders in the king's army who returned to the battle and defeated the invading force.

After the battle, the king called the general to his tent. The king told the general that for the courage he showed in saving his king he would be granted any reward he wished. Whatever he wanted would be granted, all he had to do was ask.

The general knelt before the king, removed his helmet, tore a tassel from the top and offered it to the king. Then, the general said you have already given me the greatest gift, my life.

The king looked at the tassel and remembered the night a drunken officer had dared to touch the garment of his Queen. The king now realized that drunken officer was the man kneeling before him. Through his forgiveness that night at the feast, the king had saved his own life as well. You just never know what forgiveness will bring.

You may have also heard the expression, "Forgiveness is good for the soul." To this I heartily agree, and not just the soul, but the mind and body, as well. So forgive and give others the chance to purify their energy and soul. And, you will be doing the same for yourself.

Some people have even said, "I want to be more loving, kind and forgiving. I try but I just can't. Sometimes people do things that just make me angry, there's nothing I can do about it." To this I always smile and say, "Practice more Qigong."

The energy of love, kindness and forgiveness helps to remove energy blockages in your body, to balance your energy and keep your energy flowing freely and smoothly. Practicing Qigong helps to remove energy blockages in your body, to balance your energy and keep it flowing freely and smoothly. It works both ways.

By practicing Qigong you will find that you will simply become more loving, kind and forgiving, whether you think about it or not. Whether you want to or not. It will happen and become second nature to you. It's simply the way the universe works. So many of my students have experienced this in their own lives. Ho Jun Kim's story on page 203 is a good example.

Spring Forest Qigong

I GAVE A SPEECH about Qigong a few years ago and a man came up to me afterwards and said he had been practicing Qigong for many years. He said he'd even gone to China to study and he knew that Qigong was very difficult to learn. He couldn't understand why I said Spring Forest Qigong was simple to learn. "Qigong is hard to learn," he said.

I suggested that he give Spring Forest Qigong a try and see for himself just how simple Qigong can be.

I understood very well what he was saying. For many, many years, I thought Qigong was very difficult to learn. Indeed, the way my masters taught me was very strict and difficult to learn. Some said it would take 50 years to master. Others said 20 years. Others said at least ten years. And, for them it was so. That was what they were taught.

For me, almost from the beginning of my study of

Qigong, I got a message from my sixth sense that Qigong should not be so difficult. The more I studied and practiced and advanced in Qigong the stronger this message became. Eventually, it became very clear to me that the essence of Qigong is very simple. Beautiful, powerful and yet very simple.

This is what led me to create Spring Forest Qigong. I wanted to teach Qigong so that anyone and everyone can learn it and experience the wonderful benefits for themselves.

There are thousands of different Qigong techniques in the world. They are wonderful techniques. They share the same purpose - help to awaken the healing power within each human being. But they differ in how fast and easily we can achieve the goal and how completely we can unblock the blockages in the body. Sometimes the difference is huge.

The power of Spring Forest Qigong is:

1. SFQ gives the healing power back to you.

I have met quite a few students in my classes from different states and countries who came to take my classes. They told me they had been to so many Qigong masters and teachers. When they learned their techniques, the masters very seldom explained why and how the movements can heal the body. And rarely did they teach their students how to help others to heal.

When they asked those teachers whether they could teach others the exercise, they said that is okay. But when they asked if they could help others to heal, the teachers said no. They said you have to practice for many years before you could be able to help others. They said only they could do the healing and to refer people to them. But, in my classes, I always tell people that learning to help others is simpler than learning to do the exercise to balance your own energy. You can learn to help others in just two minutes!

At the very beginning, it sounds too good to be true. But once they experience this for themselves in class, then my students agree. Everybody has this healing power. We are born with this gift. We have put it aside for a long time. Now, Spring Forest Qigong puts it back in your hands. Spring Forest Qigong helps you discover it, develop it and make good use of it.

2. SFQ requires less time and achieves more.

Qigong has four parts - the breathing; the postures; the mind; the sound. They should all work together. But some Qigong techniques focus on only one or two of these. You have to spend much longer to time to achieve what you want to fulfill. Spring Forest Qigong brings all these components together and makes good use of them, so that you spend less time and achieve more.

In my classes, many people came to talk to me that they had practiced Qigong for many years but made little progress. When they started Spring Forest Qigong, they could immediately feel the energy and healing. I know what they mean. I had walked through what they were walking through. I don't want others to spend a lot of hours or even months or years while getting little benefit.

3. SFQ reveals the truth - there is no right or wrong in Qigong movements, only good, better and best.

139

Many Qigong masters and teachers tell their students that they have to follow their instruction exactly. If not, it could cause harm in the body. So in order to learn Qigong well, you have to go to a master to learn it directly from him. Many students in my classes have asked me about this. I always smile and tell them this is not so.

You do not need "perfect" technique to benefit from Qigong. If you are practicing Qigong to help yourself there is no right or wrong only good, better and best. You simply do the best you can at that time and you will benefit. If you want to use Qigong to help others, the purity of the love in your heart and your desire to help are more important than knowing the "right" technique. You just do the best you can at that time and know that it will help your friend.

However, if you want to advance to the higher levels of Qigong to experience things many would call "super natural" then it is very important that you work with a master and follow the master's instructions explicitly. You cannot make a single mistake and it will take years to accomplish. Few people ever advance to those higher levels. But, remember, to experience the healing power of Qigong for yourself and to help others, it is not necessary to do so.

In Level One of Spring Forest Qigong, we talk about the energy channels in the body. There are twelve main channels in the body that are reflected in many points throughout the body. For example, six of these channels have points in the hands and six in the feet. When you open your hands, you help open these six channels. When you close your fingers, you close these six channels. The same thing happens when you move your feet.

When you lift your hands over your head, you help

open the lung, heart, large intestines, and many other channels. When you move your heels up and down, you help to open numerous channels, including the kidney channels where the vital life force stays. So, no matter what you do, as long as you open your hands and move your feet, you help open all these twelve channels in the body! How quickly you can get the energy to flow and the channels to open depends on how you move your hands, feet and body, the speed of the movements and the length of time you spend. This is why it's best to do your movements correctly and slowly and for as long a period of time as you can.

In Level One, one of the first movements we teach is the Moving of Yin and Yang. You put your right hand up with the fingers open and facing the upper chest, while the left hand is facing the stomach at the navel. Then, you move the hands in a circular way - the right hand moves out and down to the bottom of the torso, while the left hand moves up to the forehead. The palms of your hands should be facing the body and moving along the central line of the body. You continue moving your hands up and down in this manner.

Now here you may ask a question, what if I move my hands and they are not facing the central line of the body, is that okay? Yes. It's okay. You will still benefit from the exercise. It's just not the best. When your palms face the central line up and down along the body, you open up more channels in the same amount of time.

Here's why: In our body so many areas have responding energy points which link to various organs and other areas of the body. The following pictures show these energy points on the head, torso, hands, arms and legs. By passing energy to these points or massaging these points, you can help to open the energy blockages.

Energy Points

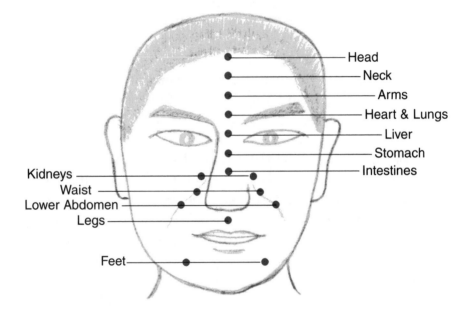

Energy Points

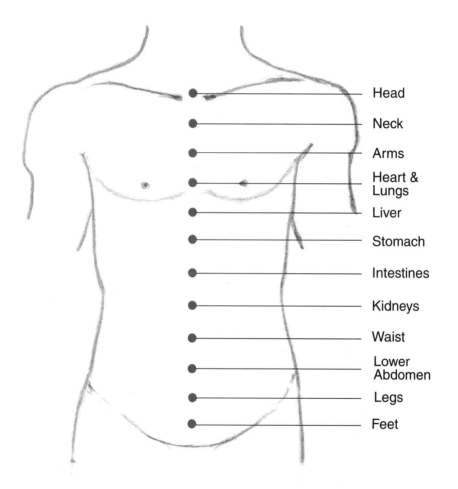

- Head
- Neck
- Arms
- Heart & Lungs
- Liver
- Stomach
- Intestines
- Kidneys
- Waist
- Lower Abdomen
- Legs
- Feet

Energy Points

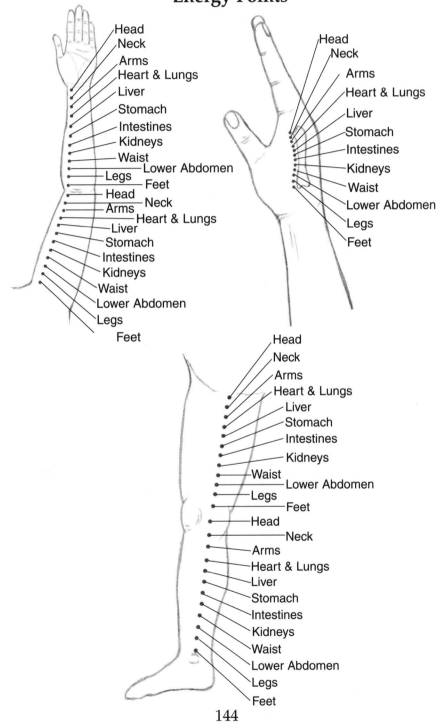

So, you see why when your hands are facing the central line you open even more responding points than moving your hands away from the central line. You get good benefit either way but one is better. And, when you open your fingers, you open all six channels in the fingers, and the responding points on the hand and on the arm also open. More benefit. Less time. Those are some of the reasons I say there is no right or wrong in your Qigong movements, just good, better and best.

I chose the name Spring Forest Qigong because of its meaning. First, think of a forest in springtime. It is so filled with new life and new growth with new beginnings and new possibilities. That is one of the reasons.

The other is that one tree does not make a forest. It takes many, many trees of many different kinds and shapes and sizes. Some very old. Some new. It takes all these to make a forest.

This is how I see Spring Forest Qigong, as one tree in the forest of helping to heal, helping to make the world a more loving place in which to live. My desire is to work with all people, with doctors and nurses and therapists and health and wellness practitioners of all kinds, with all people from all over the world, who share this same goal.

I teach four levels of Spring Forest Qigong and there is more advanced training beyond those four. However, all you need to learn to open energy blockages in your body, to balance your energy and keep it flowing freely and smoothly, you will learn in Level One. You will also learn a very simple and powerful technique for helping others and that technique I will share with you in this book.

This book is an excellent way to get started and I will teach you some valuable things to practice in this book. There are also guided meditations and other elements you should know and practice that simply can't be presented in a book. That's why I teach classes, encourage others to teach and share their knowledge with their friends and why I have created video and audio tapes to help you learn at home.

The following movements will help you get started and can be of great benefit to you.

Three Basic Spring Forest Qigong Exercises

EACH OF THESE EXERCISES, the Beginning of the Universe, the Moving of Yin & Yang, and the Breathing of the Universe, helps to open energy channels in the body and to awaken your awareness of the way the energy moves and flows through your body.

There are many energy channels in the body, but the most important ones are the front channel and the back channel. The back channel is the governing channel.

All the other energy channels work around these two main channels. One of these two main channels ends at the roof of your mouth, while the other ends at the tip of your tongue. So, whenever you practice any Spring Forest Qigong exercise you should always place your tongue gently against the roof of your mouth. Your tongue acts as the switch connecting the two main channels.

147

You can do these exercises standing, sitting, or lying down.

The Beginning of the Universe

This exercise helps bring your focus back into your body and wake up your internal energy.

• When doing this exercise while sitting, try to sit up and keep the spine straight.

• When doing this exercise while lying down, lie on your back and keep your spine as straight as possible.

• When doing this exercise while standing, stand straight with your toes pointing forward and bend your knees a little. (If you want to lose weight bend your knees a little more.)

• Set your feet a little more than shoulder width apart for good balance while standing.

• Eyes look forward.

- Wear a smile on your face to relax every part of the body and stimulate your brain to produce endorphins.

- Draw your chin back a little to straighten the entire spine. Energy travels up and down the spine in the governing channel more easily when the spine is straight.

- Drop your shoulders and move your elbows outward a little.

- Open your hands and gently spread your fingers. When you open your fingers you open many energy channels in the body. When you close your fingers you close these channels.

- Slowly take a deep, silent, gentle breath through your nose. As you breathe in, draw the lower stomach in a little. As you breathe out, let your stomach out. This makes it easier for the Yin and Yang energies to communicate with each other and create balance.

- Imagine using your whole body to breathe. Visualize the universal energy coming into every cell of your body and collecting in the lower Dantian. This is a primary energy center in your body. The lower Dantian is located in the area behind your navel.

- When you exhale, visualize any pain or sickness changing into smoke and shooting out from every cell of your body to the end of the universe.

- Gently close your eyes and lips.

- Now say the password in your mind:
  *"I am in the universe. The universe is in my body.
  The universe and I combine together."*

- Continue breathing slowly, deeply and gently and feel the emptiness, the quietness, the stillness of the universe.

Do this exercise for 2 to 3 minutes or longer if you have the time.

The Moving of Yin & Yang

This exercise is very good for healing your internal organs. Through the guidance of your mind and the movement of your hands, the heart energy and the kidney energy join during this exercise opening many blockages in the body.

Again, you may do this exercise standing, sitting, or lying down. Use the same body positions as in the Beginning of the Universe and remember to place your tongue gently against the roof of your mouth.

- Continue to breathe deeply and gently as you raise your right hand, the Yang male energy, to the upper

151

chest while you raise your left hand, the Yin female energy, to the lower stomach.

- Your hands and fingers remain slightly open to receive energy, with your palms facing your body, without touching the body, to create a sensation of emptiness.

- As you raise your hands, visualize a transparent energy column in the middle of your torso shining with beautiful colors. This energy column runs from the top of your head to the bottom of your torso. The size of the energy column depends upon your visualization. (If you have difficulty holding this visualization, don't force it. Simply say it once in your mind and then know that the energy column is there.)

- Hold this position for about 30 seconds, longer if you wish, then slowly start moving your hands. Your right hand moves out and down to the bottom of the torso while your left hand moves in and up to your face. Again, your hands do not touch your body.

- Continue moving your hands slowly in this circular pattern. Your hands move at a rate of 3 to 5 circles each minute.

- While moving your hands, visualize the energy moving up and down the transparent column and visualize the channels in the torso opening completely. (If you have difficulty holding this visualization, just say it once in your mind. Then, feel confident the transparent energy column is

152

there and focus on guiding the energy with your hands. Feel the energy moving. This is a relaxed focus. It shouldn't feel forced.)

Do this exercise for 5 to 10 minutes or longer if you can. The more time you spend doing this exercise the deeper you will start to go into the emptiness.

The Breathing of the Universe

This exercise is very good for healing the lungs and skin and to balance the energy inside and outside of the body.

If you are doing the Moving of Yin & Yang prior to doing the Breathing of the Universe you make the transition in the following way.

Finish the Moving of Yin & Yang by slowly bringing both hands to a stop in front of your navel at the position of your lower Dantian.

For men, stop with your left hand inside of your right hand. For women, stop with the right hand inside of the left hand.

Again, your hands do not touch each other or your body. This space allows you to keep the feeling of the emptiness.

- Now, focus your mind on your lower Dantian and take three slow, gentle, deep breaths.

- Then, as you inhale the fourth time, move your hands apart and open to the sides.

154

- As you exhale, bring your hands in towards each other but your hands do not touch.

- Continue doing this movement with each inhalation and exhalation, slowly and steadily.

- Imagine you are using your whole body to breathe.

- When you open your hands, feel the energy as it expands in the space between your hands.

- When you close your hands feel the energy being compressed in the space between your hands.

- With practice, and perhaps very quickly, you will actually feel the energy expanding and compressing.

- Use your hands and body to feel the energy moving while you use your elbows to guide the movements.

155

- While you inhale, visualize the pure universal energy flowing into your body through every part of your body and gathering in your lower Dantian.

- While you exhale, imagine any pain or sickness turning into smoke or air and shooting out from every part of the body to the end of the universe.

- Do not let your body sway while doing these movements. Just keep your body still and relaxed and always wear a smile on your face.

Do this movement for 5 to 10 minutes or longer if you have the time.

By moving your hands in this manner and combining the breathing technique, you help to open blockages in the whole body, especially the lungs.

When you finish this movement, stop your hands in front of you as if you were holding a ball of energy in front of your navel – your lower Dantian. Take three slow, gentle, deep breaths in through your nose.

Ending

When you are finished doing your Spring Forest Qigong exercises you should always rub your hands together and then massage your face in the following way.

Starting from the chin, gently rub your hands up your face, along the sides of your nose, up to your forehead, then out and down in a circular pattern along the sides of your face and back down to your chin. Then, start up again in the same manner. Massage your face in this way several times. Doing this helps to bring your focus back from the emptiness.

You may do these exercises in combination, one right after another; or, you can practice just one at a time. Try to practice them whenever you feel the need to completely relax and renew yourself. Even if you only have a few minutes, these exercises can be helpful. Of course, the more you practice these Spring Forest Qigong exercises and the more time you can spend doing them the more you will feel the energy and the deeper you will be able to go into the emptiness.

Always remember to say the password whenever you begin your exercises. By saying the password - *"I am in the universe. The universe is in my body. The universe and I combine together."* - you open yourself up to the universe and its limitless supply of healing energy.

Small Universe

The purpose of this meditation exercise is to clear energy blockages along the front and back channels; to physically clear the roots of sickness; and to open the energy centers along these channels.

I highly recommend this exercise. If you have time to do only one Spring Forest Qigong technique, do the Small Universe. It is extremely helpful in opening blockages and balancing all the energy in your body.

We have many energy channels and energy centers in our bodies. When energy starts at one point, visits all the channels and centers in the body, and comes back to the starting point, we have what is literally translated from ancient Chinese wisdom as a "Big Universe."

The most important energy channels are the back and

front channels in the torso. When energy starts at one point on these channels, visits all the parts of the system, and comes back to the starting point, we have what is called a "Small Universe." By focusing on moving the energy along these two main channels in the Small Universe, you have a profoundly positive effect on the Big Universe of the whole body.

The back channel starts at the lower Dantian area, which is behind the navel. It goes down to the bottom of the torso, travels up along the spine to the top of the head and comes down from the middle of the forehead stopping at the roof of the mouth. It governs all the Yang or male energy channels in the body.

The front channel also starts from the lower Dantian area, goes down to the bottom of the torso, travels up the body, passing through the heart and throat, and stopping under the tongue. It governs all the Yin or female energy channels in the body.

These two channels automatically connect together four hours a day: at midday between 11:00 a.m. and 1:00 p.m. and at midnight between 11:00 p.m. to 1:00 a.m. Qigong practitioners like to meditate at noon and midnight because it takes less energy and generates greater benefits.

Nearly all the important energy centers are arranged along the back and front channels. As a result, a blockage in the heart energy center could cause not only heart problems but problems in the lungs, breasts, chest or even mental problems. A blockage in the tailbone could cause reproductive organ problems, low sexual energy, or even headaches. A blockage in the cervical bone #7 of the spinal cord could cause headaches, fever, diabetes or even lung or heart problems.

The Small Universe is the easiest meditation technique to open these two main channels. I have created an audiotape and CD with beautiful background music and guide you through each movement in this meditation. Especially if you are a beginner, it is very difficult to do this meditation on your own.

Listen to the master's voice on the audio tape. You will hear two sounds [... O O H M ...] and [... M U A H ...].

(If you do this meditation without a tape to guide you make the "O O H M" sound with your first inhalation and visualize the universal energy flowing into your body and collecting in your Lower Dantian, which is behind your navel. As you exhale, use your mind to move the energy to the next area of your body as indicated in the picture. On the second inhalation, make the "M U A H" sound and again visualize the energy flowing into your body and collecting at this next point. Then as you exhale, use your mind to move the energy to the next area of the body. Repeat this sequence throughout the meditation.)

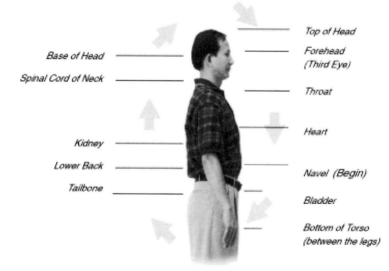

159

Helping Others to Heal

YOU CAN USE QI (energy) to heal yourself. You can also use Qi to help others to heal. The principles are the same. This is one of the most exciting and rewarding things about Qigong, helping others. It is so easy and simple to learn and yet it can be very, very helpful. This is the part I find most exciting about Spring Forest Qigong - helping others.

When you first heard that you could help others heal with your Qi, you might think this is too good to be true. Many masters also said if you want to teach how to send out Qi to help others, you have to take years of intensive training before you could do so.

When I went to my Qigong masters and asked how soon I could do healing as they did, some said ten years, some said twenty years, one even said fifty years. But my inner voice told me that healing others is even simpler than learning the Qigong exercises. I followed my inner voice and searched and searched. Now I believe I found it.

Sword Fingers

In fact, you will find it is so easy to learn this basic technique for helping others that you can learn it in just two minutes. This technique is called Sword Fingers. I teach more advanced healing techniques in my higher levels but the Sword Fingers technique is the basic one and it is very effective.

Just follow my instructions and try it today.

Sword Fingers Practice

• First hold your fingers in the Sword Fingers position. Your middle and index fingers rest together and point straight out. Your ring and little fingers are curled in towards the palm with the pad of the thumb placed over them.

• Hold up your other hand and point your Sword Fingers towards the palm of that hand just an inch or so away from it.

• Say in your mind, "Send energy out from my Sword Fingers to my palm."

161

- Keep pointing at your palm and move your Sword Fingers around in a circular motion.

- What do you feel? Feel the energy? Many people feel the energy immediately. Some take a little longer. Be paitent.

- Now, visualize there is energy like a beautiful, powerful light, shooting out of your Sword Fingers, point them at your palm and move them around again.

- Move your Sword Fingers back away from your palm about six inches and continue the circular motion.

- You can still feel the energy. You don't have to be very close. In fact, try this through a table or the back of a chair. Hold your Sword Fingers on one side and your open palm on the other. You can still feel the energy moving.

Using Sword Fingers

- Hold your fingers in the Sword Fingers position. (The tips of your little and ring fingers touch the first part of your thumb. Your middle and index fingers rest together and point straight out.)

- Put a smile on your face.

- Say the password in your mind, *"I am in the universe. The universe is in my body. The universe and I combine together."* This message opens the door to receiving the universal energy.

- Ask your friend to take three slow, gentle deep breaths and just relax. (If they want to focus on a wonderful memory or a place or something that makes them feel happy and peaceful, that is good, too.)

- Point your Sword Fingers towards an area where your friend feels pain or discomfort. (At this level you will need to ask your friend where this area is. In my advanced levels you will learn how to detect the energy blockages in the body yourself.) You do not touch your friend. You work at a distance of 6 to 18 inches away from the body. Move your Sword Fingers around to break up the energy blockages. You can move your Sword Fingers in a circular motion or in a slicing or chopping motion.

- (Do not point your Sword Fingers directly at your friend's heart. For the heart, use your Sword Fingers from the side. This is the most effective.)

- Visualize a stream of beautiful light energy coming out from your Sword Fingers and breaking up the energy blockage.

- Once you feel the energy blockage is broken up, (this should only take about 15 or 20 seconds) you need to remove the blockage.

163

- Use your hand to remove the blockage. You do this by opening your hand and visualizing energy shooting out from each of your fingers. You can use one or both hands. I recommend using only one hand.

- Visualize the energy coming out of your fingers and going into the part of your friend's body where he or she feels pain or sickness, or whatever the problem is.

- Visualize the energy changing the blockage into air or smoke. (Or feel free to be creative and use a different visualization that helps you focus the power of your mind.) Take hold of the air or smoke. Take it out of the body and throw it away. The energy blockage is simply extra energy in the body that you return to the universe. It is not bad energy, there is no such thing. It is just energy that is in the wrong place.

- Keep pulling the air or smoke out until you feel the blockage is clear. (Do not pull energy from the top of the head or from the front of the heart. This is not effective. Work on the head and the heart from the sides or from the back.)

- As you are pulling out the energy blockage it may feel stringing or sticky like spaghetti or taffy. It may feel warm or cold. People feel different sensations while doing this. Keep pulling until the sensation changes or you feel it is all gone. This should take only a minute or two, sometimes a little longer.

- While pulling out the blockage, repeat in your mind, "Blockages open. Pains are gone. You are completely healed." **Say this to yourself with great confidence and clarity.**

- When you feel the blockage is gone, you give healing energy back to the area where you removed the blockage. This helps to balance the energy and get it flowing freely and smoothly.

- Use your palm to give healing energy. (The frequency of energy from your palm is different than the frequency of the energy coming from your Sword Fingers.)

- Visualize the energy as beautiful light coming from your palm. You give energy back to the area by moving your hand in and out nine times. Always move your hands gently that way the energy will be more comforting to your friend.

- At the end, ask your friend to take three slow, gentle, deep breaths, rub her or his hands together and then massage his or her face, starting from the chin area, up along the sides of the nose to the forehead and then out and down in a circular pattern. This is the best way but don't make a big point about it. Any gentle massaging motion will be good. This helps to bring them out of their relaxed state without feeling spacey.

- Now, say to your friend, "You feel better now!" "You feel great now!" Just as you are sharing your healing energy with your friend, you want to share your positive energy and confidence. This is very helpful, too. (Don't ask, "Do you still feel the pain?" This could send the wrong message and could cause your friend to search for the pain and bring it back.)

That's it. It's just that simple. Try it and you'll see.

The more confidence you have and the clearer your focus the more effective you will be. The key is your desire to help, the love and compassion you have in your heart. This is where the healing energy comes from.

The gift of healing is one you have always had; now you know a technique to use to share this gift with your family, your friends and the whole world. From this moment on you will always know there is something you can do to help. And the more you use this technique, the more you give this gift to help others, the more your ability will increase.

Important Points

- In Spring Forest Qigong healing, the more energy you send out to heal others, the more you will receive.

- In Spring Forest Qigong we practice using the universal energy which is limitless and always available to you.

- If you are a spiritual or religious person, call upon the energy of your spiritual guides (God, Jesus, Allah, Buddha, whoever they might be). Joining their energy with yours will be even more powerful.

- Always wear a smile on your face when you are practicing Spring Forest Qigong whether for yourself or when helping others.

- The stronger your focus and visualization, the more successful your healing.

- While you are doing the healing, visualize universal energy coming into your body through every cell and gathering in your lower Dantian. (You do not have to focus on this constantly, just see it once or say it once in your mind and that will be enough.) In this way you collect more energy during the healing than you send.

- Always remember that you are helping someone else to heal themselves. The healing itself comes from the energy.

- Feel confident. Focus on how much you love people, not on success or failure. We do not control the outcome, only the effort and the message.

- Remember that it is the vibration of the energy of love, kindness and forgiveness that is healing.

- Embrace your desire to help your friend. Focus on how wonderful it is to have the opportunity to help others as you help yourself to grow and purify your own energy.

- You can use Sword Fingers to help others and you can also use your Sword Fingers to help yourself.

- This technique can be very helpful for sprains, headaches, stiffness or pain in the joints, shoulders, back or anywhere in the body, muscles aches and pains, sinus congestion, coughs, growing pains in children, stomach aches, and many, many more things.

At this beginning level you will have to ask your friend where the pain or problem is, then you can work on that specific area. It is possible there are other energy blockages in the body that are contributing to their problem.

In Level II and my more advanced classes you will learn how to locate all the energy blockages in the body and how to remove those and help your friend to balance all the energy in their body. But the Sword Fingers technique alone can be very helpful and effective.

I have shared this healing technique with thousands of people and they have been using this technique to help a lot of people, their friends, their family, even their pets and plants.

One man wrote to me from Texas. He learned the Sword Fingers technique from my Level One home study package. He used the healing technique on his mom's shoulders and knees and within a half an hour all her pain went away.

Another student, named Tina, told the class that the same night she learned the Sword Fingers technique in class she went home and found that her seven-year-old daughter had an ear infection. She tried the medicine but it did not work and her little girl was still in a lot of pain and discomfort.

So, Tina nervously tried the Sword Fingers on her daughter's ear. Within twenty minutes the pain went away and her daughter slept soundly through the night. The next morning she got up and went to school just like nothing had happened the night before.

One of my students, named Gwen, even helped her husband to get rid of very painful warts on his feet using this technique the very first day she learned it in my class. She says the warts had been a source of terrible pain for her husband for more than a year.

Another young woman told of how one of my students used this technique to help her and the next day a blemish on her nose was completely gone. She was very self-conscious about this blemish because it just wouldn't go away and no make-up would cover it. It was a small thing, but to her it was big. She thought this was a miracle. That led her to become a student.

Another student, named Joan, learned the healing technique in my class. She went home and tried it on her dog that had arthritis in the legs. When she was done, her dog got up and walked without limping.

Many students have used this simple technique to help their pets, their cats and dogs. Animals are very sensitive to this energy and find it very soothing.

Believe it or not, helping others is that simple. If you are skeptical that is okay. Many people are in the beginning. If you use the technique, you will see what happens.

I could tell you many stories, in fact you will read some of them in this book, of students who started out very skeptical, with friends and family who were even more skeptical. But, once they have the experience of Qigong healing for themselves, their doubts are gone. (Denise Douglass-White's story on page 178 or Cres Schramm's story on page 225 are good examples.)

If your friends are skeptical that is okay, too. Don't try

to convince anyone that this works. If they want you to help them, that is wonderful. If not, that is okay, too. You can still send them the energy of your love, kindness and forgiveness, in your thoughts or prayers.

Part Three

Students' Stories

"A healer in every family and a world without pain."

Students' Stories

I always leave time in my classes for my students to talk about their experiences with Spring Forest Qigong and share their stories. I love to hear their stories and it is very helpful for others. It helps them to know that Qigong really can work for anyone, not just Qigong masters.

So many students provided stories for this book that to use them all would require another volume. They are all wonderful stories and I wish we could use them all. I hope I don't hurt anyone's feelings.

We have chosen a few stories we hope will provide you with a representative sampling of experiences. Some of the stories are short. Others are long. The stories are in the student's own words and tell as much or as little as the student wanted to tell. We have presented them in alphabetical order.

We hope you enjoy them and find them meaningful to your life.

PATRICK DOUGHERTY, MA, L.P., LICENSED PSYCHOLOGIST
St. Paul, MN

Stress Relief

Spring Forest Qigong is the most remarkable and profound experience of health and healing I have ever discovered. I have searched for many, many years both personally and professionally to find ways to help myself and others bring balance and holistic health to our lives. I found what I was looking for all those years in Spring Forest Qigong.

I grew up in the suburbs of Minneapolis in a family where there was a lot of abuse and alcoholism. After high school I joined the Marine Corps and went to war in Vietnam. When I came out I spent five years working construction and living on the rougher sides of life. In those first twenty-five years of my life, I saw a lot of human tragedy.

Through all the turmoil in my life there was always a passion burning in me. I always cared about people and wanted very much to help them, but my life was such a mess and I needed so much help myself I couldn't imagine how I would ever be able to do anything to help others. It wasn't until I went through treatment for alcohol and drug addiction back in 1976 that a door opened for me to start doing something for other people.

In the late 70's I did some work in chemical dependency and then in 1981 I went over and lived in Northern Ireland for half a year working with a peace and reconciliation retreat center. That's where I formulated most of my thoughts for my master's degree. I came back and got my Master's in Psychology, in human development, got my

173

psychology license and went into private practice.

I have always loved my work but have always been very frustrated by how long it takes for people to heal. People come with a myriad of problems, from marital discord to past trauma, to anxiety and depression, to feeling lost in their lives. Most of the time they want to talk about it, do the traditional psychotherapy approach. Quite often, it is their whole life that needs attention.

Clients come to me because of mental health problems but frequently they aren't doing enough to maintain their physical or spiritual health either. They are very out of balance in mind, body and spirit. They come hoping that talking about and understanding their problems, and maybe getting in touch with their feelings about their problems, will get them in touch with their vital health and spiritual path. Obviously, that usually doesn't happen. Psychotherapy ends up to be so often a very slow and often incomplete healing process for what the client is seeking.

So many of the problems people come to me for could be so much more quickly remedied if they were engaging their bodies energetically and working on their spiritual lives. The clients that have sought physical and spiritual balance as well as working on their mental health are the clients that usually progress the fastest and have the most profound healing. So I've encouraged people for years to do Tai Chi, Yoga, body work, meditation, anything, just do something besides talk about it.

I have tried many of these approaches and practiced some of them for years but have always known why so many of my clients were balking at my suggestions. They weren't prepared to do the years of practice most of these approaches would require to feel a significant benefit in their life. And I knew they were right, that is, until I found Spring Forest Qigong.

One December when I was especially tired and stressed out with work, two young kids, a marriage and all the complexities of life, I called up this friend of mine who was also wandering all over the place searching for a better life and we had lunch. I said, "Jim, I'm tired. I'm stressed out. My practice is feeling pretty boring. I'm tired all the time and feel like my life is a grind. I've just been reading about this stuff call Qigong. There's a class down at the community ed center. Some guy's offering two two-hour classes that he promises can change your life. You ever heard of that stuff?"

Jim said, "You know, if you're going to study Qigong, you might as well study with a Chinese Qigong master." I said, "Right, Jim, where am I going to find one of those up here in the frozen tundra of Minnesota." And he said, "Anoka Ramsey Junior College, about 20 minutes away." I didn't need a spiritual director to point out the clear message for me to follow this path.

So, he handed me Chunyi Lin's phone number and I called him up and he said, "Yes, I have a class starting Wednesday night." And I said, "Oh, I'm going to be out of town. Can I start the week after?" He said, "No. You can start next month." I said, "Oh, boy, I'm really supposed to start now. What can I do?" And he said, "I'm sorry." So that Wednesday as I drove out of town a snowstorm drove in right behind me and he canceled his first class. So I called him up when I got home and he said, "Yes, class will start this Wednesday. Come." I did and my life hasn't been the same since.

With that first class I knew immediately that Qigong had power that other modalities did not because I could feel something different. Then in just two or three weeks I could literally feel the energy. I could feel a lot of it. I first thought that there was some external breeze around my head. Master Lin told me it was energy. Then it would move around my head and then inside my head and then move down my spine. So I knew my Qigong practice was having an impact on me energetically, it was so reinforcing. It was working and I could feel it. So, I began to practice a lot.

Around my house, my family could feel it. My wife kept saying, "What's going on with you? You seem so much more relaxed?" I wasn't feeling stressed anymore.

Just about all of us know that stressed feeling. It's like your energy's sort of pushing out six different directions and you can't get enough sleep and you come home and you just want to sit in front of the tube and not think about anything. I didn't have that anymore. I just didn't have that stressed feeling anymore. It is humbling to look back and see the level of mental health I was accepting as normal. That is no way to live.

It was interesting being at a party, being out with friends when they got to talking, "Oh, I'm so stressed because I'm doing this and I'm doing that and my kids are involved with this event and you know what it's like." And everyone else is going, "Mmhmm, oh, yeah." And I'm going, "I'm sorry. Yeah, I'm doing all that stuff too but I just don't feel stressed anymore."

That happened very early in my practice. Like three months probably into the process of learning and practicing Spring Forest Qigong I could just feel everything was changing. Rather than going to bed earlier, I was going to bed later because I was staying up and practicing. I was getting up earlier and practicing. I couldn't practice enough. I was practicing every morning and every night. So that was very, very good and my sleep got a lot better.

I was always a light sleeper. I was part of the twenty percent of America that has some form of insomnia and now I sleep like a baby, and I need less sleep. It's very, very good for the sleep. It's all due to practicing Spring Forest Qigong.

I think the key to the whole thing is breathing. When you learn how to breathe and breathe with the right images in your mind, your breath can change and your life can change. If people just learned the breath work and if you gave people just three of the Qigong exercises that focused on the breath, that alone could significantly change their lives. It is that simple.

I teach classes to psychotherapists now, Spring Forest Qigong for psychotherapists, and that's what I teach them. They can give their clients so much help by just teaching them a little Qigong. They have to practice Qigong of course for them to be effective models. They have to get their own breath work right. But they learn like I did that getting your own self in balance, opens up the door for healing on all levels, body, mind and spirit. Then you can teach your clients one or two simple breathing exercises and some visualization techniques and it can so enhance their healing.

One of the things I've learned from Master Lin and Spring Forest Qigong is that it is very simple to change your life. In Level 1 he tells us everything we need to know is here in this course. It is so simple. I have taken all the levels he offers and have found that he told the truth back in Level 1. A focused, consistent and simple practice can have the most profound impact on your body, mind and spirit.

DENISE DOUGLASS-WHITE
St. Croix Falls, Wisconsin

Healing Myself, My Children and Others

I wandered into my first Spring Forest Qigong class. My friend had just started a Level I class taught by Master Lin and invited me to join her. I didn't know anything about Qigong. I thought it was some sort of Chinese exercise program that would benefit me through physical exercise, maybe a little meditation thrown in. I had never done any energy work, can't say that I was even aware of energy work and had never meditated before.

After I began my class and discovered Spring Forest Qigong had to do with healing, both receiving and giving, I worked to keep an open mind, but my logical, western cultural orientation anchored me solidly as a skeptic. Little did I realize I had just taken the first steps in a remarkable journey that would change my life.

The changes that have taken place within me haven't been influenced by an epiphany event in my thinking, but a series of events that have individually forced me to address the way that I define not only my health and the health of others but the way I see and think about my world. I'll share with you a few of the events the universe has placed in my path.

While taking my Level I class, I had toyed with the idea that Spring Forest Qigong (SFQ) healing might be like a sugar placebo. Perhaps it could work in cases where the people weren't "really" sick, but had only psychologically convinced themselves they were sick. Since they weren't really sick in the first place, SFQ could be used with them successfully as the person "unconvinced" themselves, thereby mimicking "real" healing.

178

For several years my son had been coming down annually with bronchitis which quickly progressed to pneumonia. It had a very predictable pattern. He would start experiencing cold-like symptoms, light congestion, then almost immediately it would come on hard and fast like the flu, move to his lungs with massive congestion and coughing on the level of bronchitis, and finally turn to pneumonia.

This night before I left for my Level I Qigong class, my son had started into this pattern. He was feeling miserable; the heavy congestion had started to move into his lungs. I returned from class and my son was asleep in his bed. His breathing was labored. I went in without waking him and "balanced his yin & yang" just as I had practiced in class that night then went to bed.

When we awoke in the morning he yelled upstairs to me, "Mom, my lungs are totally clear" and they were. I was surprised and delighted that my son was well, and decided that SFQ couldn't possibly be only a placebo idea, because my son didn't know what I was doing in my class and wasn't awake when I worked on him. I didn't really have an explanation for what occurred. I was pleased yet a little uneasy.

I struggled with concerns that Qigong might connect me with something, larger than I could understand or control, which had the possibility of being not only good but also evil. I asked myself if Qigong matched my understanding of what a cult was. I wondered if with all his command of that which I did not understand if possibly Master Lin could gain control of my mind or will.

For several years I had been having problems with my liver. The doctors weren't able to tell me exactly what was wrong. I had several elevated liver tests. The doctors said

179

they suspected Gilber's Syndrome. They said they couldn't do much, they just tested my liver levels regularly to make sure they didn't elevate further. My symptoms were mostly fatigue.

One day, during my Level II class, we were practicing our movements. Master Lin, often worked with all of his student's energies during this time. On this occasion, he came behind me and began working with mine. All of a sudden, over my liver area, I felt what seemed like a giant bubble of pressure bursting and disappearing out my back. It felt so good to no longer have this pressure there, yet I didn't even know I had any pressure there until it was gone. Believe me, it was very real.

Shortly, after this class I went in for my scheduled tests and I thought I knew what they would find. In fact, one of the tests was totally normal and the other was nearly normal. The doctor said he couldn't really explain it. I was thrilled, I was not surprised, but the facts of what occurred did not fit into my understanding of the universe nor my belief system. When I think back, it amazes me that something miraculous like that happened and yet I still couldn't accept it for what it was. I wasn't ready yet.

During my Level III Class, a very dear loved one who lived out of state, had a seizure. The doctors indicated one of several possibilities, either a tumor, an embolism or an infection in her brain. I talked to Master Lin about it after class one day. He said that it was a brain tumor, in fact he said there were two, and very matter of factly, he proceeded to draw me a diagram of where each was located. I was totally blown away. The idea that someone could actually detect illness from long distance was so phenomenal that it actually scared me.

I was so moved by love for this person that I asked

Master Lin if he would work with her long distance. He agreed and also instructed me as to how I could help. I called and talked to my loved one. I asked her where the doctors said the brain problem was. She described exactly one of the places that Master Lin had indicated. I did as he said. When they did follow up testing on my loved one, the doctors could no longer detect anything wrong with her brain.

Through the course of time I was learning to trust the guidance of this gentle and very good man. He helped me to slowly begin to accept. Yet, just when I became accepting of one thing, I would be exposed to another level of being astounded.

With almost no forewarning my mother was diagnosed with Glioblastoma Multiforme- a level 4 (the worst) cancerous brain tumor. I had Master Lin work with her long distance several times but he was clear that the help he could provide would not cure her of the disease- it was too far along. It was a difficult time for my family. Although Mom was very open to Qigong treatment, other family members were not. It was hard being directly faced with, and operating at the juncture of two separate belief systems, that which I had been brought up with and that, which was evolving for me.

At the end of my mom's life, we provided hospice care in my home and were her primary caregivers. Her death in our home was not what I expected. The end was very difficult. For hours she gasped for breath, like a marathon runner at the end of a race, worn out and exhausted. It was torturous to watch this remarkably kind and wonderful woman having to use the last of her human strength to fight yet another final battle.

As I witnessed, the process of her transition I felt

moved to help her with Qigong yet was unsure if I should intervene. My brother and sisters were present in the room, so I didn't want to use movement, as it seemed invasive. I decided to place my hand on her chest and silently asked for help for my mom. Almost immediately, her breathing began to slow down, her body relaxed and she died.

My poor little belief system was becoming riddled like a pincushion. Something needed to change. Time and time again the universe asked me to open my mind. I began to open my mind to a whole new way of thinking-body, mind and spirit.

I learned to meditate. I read about anatomy and physiology. I learned to detect energy blockages in people's bodies. I researched Qigong. I began to respect my own body in a new way that caused me to choose more exercise, better nutrition, elimination of harmful substances, regular meditation and to make changes in my lifestyle that would reduce stress and increase the balance I need in my life.

Last fall, a friend who is a duella (assists in births) asked me to help one of her clients whose baby was in breech position. I asked another Qigong friend to help and we worked long distance with this woman over the weekend. Both my friend and I had a strong sense that this fetus was a girl. On Monday morning the pregnant woman went into the doctor for a procedure to manually turn the baby but they discovered the baby had already turned.

The duella friend asked me to help with another client whose baby was breech. Again, my friend and I worked with the woman. Again the baby turned. Again we had an unasked for sense of the baby's gender, this time a boy.

The babies delivered. The first was a girl and the second was a boy, just as we detected.

Over the holidays, my family and I visited my sister-in-law out of state. She has had regular migraine headaches for years. She had a really bad one when we were there. She took her medication in the morning but it didn't help. I offered to provide Qigong therapy. She accepted and after I worked with her, her headache was totally eliminated. She was dumbfounded. I smiled.

I'm working with a young boy now who has a congenital heart defect. I had the most remarkable meditation that showed me a clear picture of an event from one of his past lives. I had just barely begun to think about the possibility of past lives before this message was placed before me. I was startled, a little shaken, but accepting.

This story still unfolds, yet I am certain that I am where I should be. I am healthier and stronger than I have been in decades. I have grown spiritually. I feel grateful to the loving relationships I have with my family and friends. I am forever in debt to Master Chunyi Lin. He has opened my eyes, mind and spirit to the connectiveness of all life, to the miracle of our lives and the unlimited potential we have as human beings.

I work now as a volunteer for the Spring Forest Qigong Association. I listen to the stories of others like myself and am continually moved to tears, at the number of people that Chunyi Lin has both directly and indirectly effected, by helping to improve their health and their lives. In the short time span of about five or six years, modest, unassuming, quiet, gentle, good humored Master Lin, has brought Spring Forest Qigong to this country, not only changing my life, but impacting the lives of hundreds of his students. His work continues to ripple out through his student's work to positively impact the lives of thousands.

After five years of involvement with Spring Forest Qigong I can say that I have seen enormous good come from the practice of Spring Forest Qigong healing. I have observed no evil, in fact I feel protected from evil through my association with Spring Forest Qigong. Chunyi Lin has no evil intent and Spring Forest Qigong is nothing like a cult.

Spring Forest Qigong has provided an opportunity for me to stretch beyond my understanding of the world in which I live, to explore the furthest reaches of my human potential. I consider myself proof that any average person can learn SFQ, no matter how slow they are to assimilate the lessons placed in their path. I feel privileged, blessed and lucky to have wandered into that first SFQ class to learn from Master Chunyi Lin.

TOM GOW
Two Harbors, Minnesota

Bone Marrow Disease

I was diagnosed with aplastic anemia and myelodis-plasia in December of 1998. I tried many different treatments and my doctor recommended a bone marrow transplant. We held many bone marrow drives up here but I didn't find a suitable donor. Out of 500 who were tested, only my sister and half-brother were a half-match, but that's only a forty-percent chance of success.

I'm a letter carrier and have been for 17 years. I walk five miles a day on my route and when I was first diagnosed I didn't go back to my route for six months. Then when I did go back to work by the time I got home I was pretty pooped. It was on to the couch I'd go.

One Saturday in October of 1999, I was out on my route and ran into a fella named Tom Sullivan. He asked me if I'd found a donor yet and I said no. Then he told me about this man, Chunyi Lin, who teaches this healing called Spring Forest Qigong. Tom had already been through Levels 1 through 4.

I'd never heard of it so he told me what it was all about and gave me Chunyi's number and I gave him a call. To the Western mind it's not easy to accept because if it can't be seen, touched or measured, it's not real. But, I'm open to pretty much anything and I learned with the Qigong it goes back thousands of years so there's got to be something to it.

I made an appointment and drove down to see him. I went to his home and I walked in and explained what was going on and I sat down and he did his thing. Then as I was leaving, just as I had my hand on the door, he said, "Oh, by the way Tom, your back will feel better tomorrow."

I hadn't said anything to him about my back. That was the least of my problems. But, by golly, it did and I haven't been to a chiropractor since. I used to go to the chiropractor all the time. I'd stop in on my route in the morning. I'd be in his office by 10 a.m. and my back would be out again by 12:30 and that went on for two or three years. But, not anymore since that first treatment with Chunyi. And, I do the Spring Forest Qigong myself now, of course. I get a ping once in a while but I just do my Qigong and like that it's just gone.

The first two times I went to see Chunyi I didn't notice too much of a difference besides my back being okay and all that. But, the third time down I went, "Whoa." That was a burst of energy. I felt great.

I got home that night after driving down there and back, about a five hour drive, and I worked in the barn until about 11 o'clock. And, I've been pretty much having a lot of energy since then. That wouldn't have been possible before. My oncologist is surprised I'm still doing my route. In fact, my oncologist is so impressed he's sent patients to see Chunyi. And, since doing the Qigong, I don't hit the couch anymore. It's just go, go, go.

I keep a pretty heavy schedule here. I'm a very active 4-H leader still. I've got 34 kids this year. I'm saddle club president and a union officer in our union and a union steward and a County Fair board member. In the winter, I coach basketball.

We have two kids, sixteen and twelve. We have a little 13-14 acre farm and keep four horses. We're into horses, fast horses and gaming events on horses. I give my 4-H kids free horse back riding lessons and let them ride my horses in competition for two years. There's always lots of chores to do. Been doing some remodeling around here. Put a new bathroom in this winter. So, I put in long days.

I've taken all the Spring Forest Qigong levels now and I try to get at least a half hour of the meditations or exercises in each day. With the Qigong I've found I can power up when I have to.

I do healings up here too now and I have a pretty steady clientele. I don't charge anything and I have a pretty good success rate. People keep coming to see me. Everything from fibromyalgia to stroke, bad backs, that's pretty common, people with a lot of stress. I'd say about 97-precent of them get relief for anywhere from three days to three months. I even give my horses treatments before they go out to run and it makes a difference.

I just recently got back from seeing my bone marrow doctor and he can't believe how well I'm doing. In fact, he can't believe I'm still alive. Ninety-percent of the patients who have the same thing I do, who have damage to the same chromosome I do, die within the first year. My bone marrow doctor has never had a patient who survived longer than three years, except for me. It's been more than four years for me and I'm still going strong.

If you ask me where I'd be without the Spring Forest Qigong, I probably wouldn't be here. If I was here, I probably wouldn't be able to work. Couldn't do all the things I do now, that's for sure. That Qigong has really been the ticket I think.

Qigong has allowed me to maintain a very high quality of life physically, mentally and spiritually. I always look forward to seeing Chunyi. He charges my batteries up like the energizer bunny.

187

For people who doubt it I just say try it. You've got nothing to lose.

DARCIE GUSTINE GRIM
Stillwater, MN

Chronic, Debilitating Pain

It was October 30th, 1993, when I finally spoke with a doctor about my on-going headache. I started with the nurse, telling her I needed help; I was in great pain. She asked me to document my headaches and she would set up an appointment for me in two weeks. I explained to her that I had been documenting my headaches and they had moved from their usual seven to ten day adventures to even longer periods of time. I had officially begun counting the days as of October 1st, so the headache I was experiencing had been tormenting me for at least thirty consecutive days. The nurse gave me the doctor to speak to. I saw her two days later.

Headaches ran in the family so I naturally thought they were simply a part of life rather than my body telling me there was something wrong. I had experienced long stints of headaches since I was thirteen with regular frequency. I remember a pattern of weeklong headaches with a two-week break throughout my tenth grade year, increasing to ten days of a headache with a one-week break between. I had spoken to doctors, but headaches were simply a part of my history and my family's history as was a high threshold of pain, and I was tough.

Of course, the type of headache I had was diagnosed as a stress headache because my neck muscles were so tight they felt like they could replace any stringed instrument. The handfuls of aspirin and ibuprofen I had been self-medicating with were useless.

I was put through eight weeks of biofeedback to document the fact that I was able to relax myself even though my headache raged on. I spent at least six months in physical therapy, which gave me a sense of reduced pain, lasting, if I was lucky, about thirty minutes after each session. I was given a bottle of something that I could literally freeze my neck with to numb the pain as I did stretching exercises. Unfortunately, my headache continued.

The general practitioner had referred me to a neurologist who had prescribed the physical therapy as well as a variety of medications. One of these drugs, I had to shoot myself in the leg with. It didn't help much and it raced my heart. I remember painfully sitting up in the living room one night so that I could be around another human being who would be able to call 911 in case I suffered a heart attack. My heart was beating so fast and hard that I was terrified.

Finally, I was prescribed a very scary, highly addictive drug. I took the maximum dosage I could take without any relief. When this did not succeed, I had my last appointment with my neurologist where she informed me that I had received all the help that could be offered in the field of traditional western medicine. She could continue looking for a drug that would mask my pain, but the cause of my headaches was unknown. I was unhelpable.

Fortunately, I became angry about this diagnosis of futility. I knew I was not going to live such an unbearable life of pain. I had already decided exactly what I would do if I ran out of hope, but until then, I would pursue every avenue of possibility out there. Since traditional western medicine could not help me, I would find help elsewhere. I began my journey into the field of alternative health.

I read a book by Deepak Chopra and called a man I

190

found on a reference list in the back of this book who worked in St. Paul. He was also a chiropractor. He looked at my x-rays and told me that my pain made perfect sense. I practiced some Maharishi Ayurveda and was gently adjusted by this kind-hearted chiropractor. I was finally able to experience my first totally pain free moment over the course of an entire year, after receiving a chiropractic adjustment. After these adjustments I would be headache free for the remainder of the day and sometimes even part of the following day. I was scheduled for two appointments per week.

During the next few months, my headaches had changed from one continuous headache to daily bouts lasting approximately five hours. However, the rest of my body was acting up, and it was with great difficulty that I was able to walk. It seemed as though my whole spinal structure was in revolt as were all the muscles that were attached to it. I began seeing a massage therapist twice a week as well. I was in such pain; I shuffled like an old lady when I walked.

It was an arduous task bringing my students down the hall to the lunchroom or to other classes. My hand shook as though I had epilepsy when I held up flash cards in math. I feared the intense pain that would hit me every day at one o,clock, starting the next marathon headache. My quality of life was nonexistent. Every ounce of energy I had was going into surviving the pain. I was utterly exhausted. I finally hit the wall in December of 1994 and had to take a medical leave of absence from my teaching position.

I saw the state's doctor who examined me and recommended that I receive unemployment compensation. I was also examined by an independent orthopedic doctor and licensed chiropractor who thoroughly examined me and wrote a five page paper explaining all my body's impediments and diagnosed me with fibromyalgia tendencies. In fact, one of my appointments with this man was on my thirtieth birthday. I was in unexplainable pain. It took a tremendous amount of effort to endure it.

My occipital area of my head was actually inflamed. The doctor was acutely aware of the type of pain I must be experiencing. He offered to take a very long needle and insert some medication to numb the pain by going under and up into my skull. He was thoroughly shocked when I declined this assistance which he offered three or four times.

You see, this by far, was not the first time I had experienced this kind of intense pain. It was simply the only time a doctor had actually seen me in the throws of it. I had dealt with this pain on my own without help many, many times. Anyway, this doctor's recommendation was that I should be placed on permanent state assistance for the remainder of my life because he saw the severity of my condition and knew of no means in which to correct it. Again, I was only thirty years old.

I was at a plateau and so I looked for more help. A dear friend of mine recommended me to a network chiropractor named Carol Jillian. She was truly an answer to prayer. You see, I was thousands of dollars in debt to family members because my insurance did not cover massage or continuous chiropractic adjustments. Doctor Jillian charged a flat fee. I could see her as many times a week as I wanted. I saw her four times a week for the first two to three years.

I had gone back to working full time the following school year despite the orthopedic/chiropractic doctor's

192

recommendation. The students were very compassionate, and I gave them all my energy. I was in horrendous pain in the evening and prayed each morning that I would make it through the day. It was by sheer determination and heavenly assistance that I made it through this period of time in my life.

Fortunately. my body was responding to this new healing modality offered by Dr. Jillian and my intense pain decreased over the years. I was given strategies and new understandings on how to live life and assist my body with its healing, but I wanted even more. I asked Dr. Jillian if she knew this man named Chunyi Lin who was offering Qigong classes at Anoka-Ramsey. She gave him high praise and encouraged me to go.

I was already open to Chinese healing because I had also seen a Chinese herbalist who told me that my history of ailments in my life were easily explained by the philosophy of Chinese medicine. What I had been through and was dealing with currently made sense. I was not a mystery case or a lost cause, but rather a pretty classic case through the eyes of Chinese medicine. I responded well to the medicinal herbs and recommendations. I avoided gall bladder surgery, and I wasn't quite so exhausted all the time. I was still in a pretty big mess though, when I attended my first class with Master Lin in August of 1997, but I had actually made a long, exhausting advancement in my health to get there. He gave me hope and I was so utterly needy. My heart ached ... my soul ached. I wanted a better quality of life. When I was in high school, my friends use to tease me about the fact that I smiled all the time. I had a bubbly, positive attitude, and I loved to hand out hugs. This part of me had disappeared completely. I was so beaten down with pain; I found it difficult to look into people's eyes. I felt as though I were in a very deep, dark pit, trying to climb my way out of it.

I hungrily gobbled up what Master Lin taught. It was new to me, but this Chinese philosophy of life made sense. I could easily apply it to my life experiences. I felt stronger and happier. I could even make the pain I would wake up writhing with in the middle of the night go away using one of the exercises taught in his Level One class. I listened to and practiced the Small Universe lying down in bed because sitting up was too hard. I felt like a horrible student, but I did a lot more than I gave myself credit for at the time. I realize now that my kidney energy was so depleted that concentrating on the Small Universe meditation as I did was perfect for me.

I immediately signed up for Level Two. During this time, my mom was dealing with breast cancer. She elected to have a double mastectomy, but was extremely fearful of all of this because she had not yet recovered from a very traumatic kidney surgery. My mom had donated a kidney to my sister and it did not go well for my mom. Three years later, she was still experiencing a lot of painful discomfort. She did not know how she could possibly deal with this pain along with the pain of her upcoming surgery. My mom had always been healthy so the last couple years had been very difficult for her.

I was so concerned about my mom that I was compelled to heal her with Qigong. I worked on her every night a week before the surgery. During this time, the pain she usually felt and had felt over the last couple years had completely disappeared. This comforted her greatly. She went into surgery much more relaxed. I worked on her every day in the hospital and also did some long distance healing when she chose to stay with my aunt a week after she returned home from the hospital. My mom became my greatest ally of Spring Forest Qigong. I was given the opportunity to put into practice what I had learned about healing others and to see the results for myself. It truly was amazing.

Some of my family thought I was absolutely weird and teased me about this Voodoo stuff I did. I simply smiled. I knew what I knew. I had been through the ringer and found a healing path that would and has changed my life dramatically. With my lack of concern for converting my siblings to my way of thinking and my mom exclaiming her miraculous experiences, my family opened themselves to alternative possibilities, and I continued learning.

One of the first bits of feedback I ever received when healing someone else was from my nephew, Jacob. He was approximately nine years old at the time. We were spending the day together, but unfortunately, Jacob had a headache. He did have some water with him, so I passed some energy into the water with a message to relieve him of his headache. I had him drink some of the water and then close his eyes and relax. As he was resting, I concentrated on breaking up the blockages in his head. I was trying to heal him without him realizing that I was doing something different when his eyes popped open, and he whipped his head to the left to face me. He said it was gone and asked with great conviction what I had done to make it go away. I was just beginning my training with Spring Forest Qigong so I was as surprised as my nephew was. It was evident, however, what I was learning truly worked.

After that, I had the confidence, desire, and opportunity to heal my mom as I shared earlier. So I continued training and practicing Spring Forest Qigong and was working with the concept of psychic surgery when I received a tearful phone call from my mom who had just learned that her only brother was diagnosed with tumors on his adrenal glands. There was great concern that the tumors were cancerous and the cancer was spreading throughout the body. The other concern was that the surgery was rather precarious because if the adrenal gland was cut into, chemicals could be released in the body and that could be very damaging to my uncle.

Both of my mom's parents had died from cancer so my mom was terrified for my uncle. She was panicked and grief stricken when she called. My reaction, however, was calm, and I had a feeling of empowerment because I knew exactly how I could help my uncle. So I told my mom what I would do and encouraged her to do her own healing meditation for my uncle as well. I emphasized that meditation was much more powerful than tears and how she would truly be helping her brother if she chose this course of action instead. She calmed down and asked me to call her sister and tell her the same thing, so I did. Then, I meditated.

In my healing meditation, I pictured my uncle's adrenal glands with the tumor on top of them which I pictured encapsulating into a ball with a skin around it so the doctors who were doing surgery could easily see that the tumor had in no way spread beyond the adrenal glands. Then I asked the universe to place some fatty tissue between the tumor and the adrenal glands so that removing the tumor would be easy for the doctors. My third request was for a spiritual healing prompting my uncle to take this experience as an omen and retire from his job a year early rather than going back to a stressful situation. When I finished my meditation, I was completely at peace and felt confident that my uncle would be absolutely fine. I went on my vacation. Every time I checked in on my uncle in meditation, I received the same feeling that he was fine.

When I returned from my vacation, my mom called to let me know that my uncle was indeed doing well, the surgery had been a breeze, but it had been very unusual. When the doctors had opened him up, they found the tumors in nice round packages with a sort of skin around them, which was surprising. Even more so, however, was the nice bit of fatty tissue connecting each tumor to its corresponding adrenal gland so that there was no concern of damaging the glands in any way when the tumors were removed.

Then my mom said that my uncle had decided to take this whole experience as an omen and chose to retire from his job a year early. Wow! Everything I had asked for and pictured in my healing meditation came to fruition. I was so blown away by this that it took me three months to share this story with my friends, and I still have never spoken to my uncle about it. I had never worked with energy healing before learning Spring Forest Qigong, and I didn't feel like any kind of a guru or expert when this healing took place, so I am certain that anyone can do this kind of healing work if they come from a place of love.

I really enjoy helping people. I have been given several opportunities to work with others and have seen wonderful results. I have helped several people with headaches. One person I worked with had been suffering from headaches over the past seventeen years. After two recently grueling surgeries, which were deemed unsuccessful, I worked with him for a period of time. His headaches stopped.

Other healings I've assisted with, however, were more in regards to the spirit of the heart. I have witnessed a kind of personality change where life is taken in and lived with a greater ease or balance. This is also true of my own life.

I have been studying Spring Forest Qigong since 1997. I am virtually pain free through the practice of the active exercises and meditation. I have a very deep belief that Spring Forest Qigong works and have witnessed the healing of others that I've worked with. I am very thankful for what I've learned from the pain I experienced. I think, feel, and act much differently than I use to.

Now, when I look at my own behavior and actions I look to see if they reflect a healer's heart of love, kindness, and forgiveness. Needless to say, my actions have been noticeably different to those around me and to myself as well. Spring Forest Qigong has healed me physically, emotionally, and spiritually. I like myself and feel much more at peace. People tell me I radiate an inner enthusiasm for Spring Forest Qigong and contentment of life.

This is true. My joy and smile have returned.

MICHAEL HACKETT
Eden Prairie, MN

Depression and Balance

I cannot say enough good things about Master Chunyi Lin. He is amazing. He is the only person I have ever met who loves others unconditionally and does not judge anyone around him. He lives the happiness and contentment that I believe we are all searching for. It's right there in his heart and it shows on his face. I just thank God that I am so fortunate to know Master Lin.

I am the last person I ever thought would be studying some ancient Chinese practice called Qigong. But thank God I found it. I don't think I would be here today; I certainly wouldn't be in this good health, this good form, this happy, if it wasn't for Spring Forest Qigong.

I grew-up on a dairy farm in Ireland, a good, Irish Catholic, God-fearing soul. I got my work ethic and strength from my father and my belief in God and Christianity from my mother. My father suffered from depression for many years and it was a terrible thing to see.

I was a grown man and married when I finally came to the realization that I suffered from depression as well. I felt sick for many years before I was willing to acknowledge that I had a problem. About six years ago, I started seeking treatment for my depression and the panic attacks I would suffer. A doctor put me on a medication that was very successful but did not really solve my problem. My marriage began to fail and the depression got worse.

I have seen many different counselors and therapists and while I found all of it to be valuable it still didn't solve my problem and my marriage ended in divorce.

I work as an arborist and spend a lot of my days climbing trees to prune and shape them. I found my balance starting to suffer about two years ago and often became terrified when climbing. I didn't know what to do. Then, I just happened to be reading a magazine and there was this story about Spring Forest Qigong and it said something about "balance" or "life balance" in the magazine. And I thought if this is going to help me with my equilibrium then I'm going to go. So, I enrolled in this class in Spring Forest Qigong.

When I got there it wasn't all what I expected. For one thing, most of the other students were women, which made me feel pretty awkward. I thought, "Oh, cripes, this must be a woman's thing. I'm in the wrong class." But, as soon as I saw Master Lin, as soon as he started to talk, I knew I'd come to the right place.

I was so desperate to find answers at that point, to find balance, and not just for working in the trees but balance in my life. The truth was I wanted to find happiness. I wanted to know where happiness comes from and everything Master Lin said just spoke right to my heart. As I thought about what he said it all just seemed like such common sense.

When Master Lin teaches that the power of Qigong comes from love and forgiveness and sending that love and forgiveness to yourself and to everyone, it just made so much sense to me. That's what life is really all about. That's where happiness and contentment can be found. You could just see the happiness and contentment in the man's face. He was living proof.

Practicing the Spring Forest Qigong techniques I learned from Master Lin totally changed my life. That happiness and peacefulness just blossomed inside me. Even with all that I still never thought that I could detect blockages in someone else's body and help them to heal themselves like he said I could. But, I kept practicing and it's happening. I can do it. And, I know you can too. And, I'll tell you what it feels like. You know when you have a great dinner and then you have that vanilla ice cream for desert and it just tastes so good. That's what it's like.

When I do the exercises or I do a meditation now, just go into the emptiness like Master Lin teaches and not force it, just wait for it to come and that peacefulness always comes. It's almost like the mind goes to sleep and the spirit comes awake. I meditate and just the weight of the world leaves my shoulders and when I open my eyes it's just happiness and contentment. And to me, I think it's just a stairway to heaven.

If you ask me where I'd be without Spring Forest, I'd still be the hotheaded Irishman I've always been. And I probably would have gone through at least a couple of jobs by now. I would probably be like I was two years ago, just a hotheaded workaholic who consistently turned around and blamed pretty much everyone else for my problems, for my mistakes. I think that's where I would be if I was still alive, because I came pretty close to just taking off, just getting rid of myself. So, without Spring Forest Qigong I'd be here or I might not be here but I'd be in a hell of a mess.

I'd done a lot of work before I came to Spring Forest Qigong, but Spring Forest Qigong was just like the icing on the cake. It's just like having a key to unlock a door and inside there are one or two or three tools and you just take them out and you use them. You use them and you can literally take yourself down the path of happiness.

But, they're just tools. No one can use them for you. You have to do it for yourself.

Without a doubt in my heart, Spring Forest Qigong will work for anybody who consistently puts forth the effort to do a little Spring Forest Qigong meditation, a little exercise for themselves. You may not always feel like doing it, but, by golly, you go ahead and do it and it will pay you ten-fold.

HO JUN KIM
Houston, TX

From Alcoholism to Enlightenment

I wasn't looking to change my life. I wasn't looking to study Qigong, but I did and it changed my life. I didn't even want my life to change but it did.

I like to drink. I've always liked to drink. I like to drink beer, wine, and hard liquor. I started drinking when I was in high school. Even then I would have a couple of shots of liquor every day before going to school. I like to drink a lot.

I also love hot, spicy food, the hotter the better. I'm Korean, born in Seoul and grew-up in south Texas. So, I love hot food. I also love salty food. I'd salt everything. I had a girlfriend once who tried to get me to use this light salt. I went out and bought her real salt. I couldn't eat that other stuff.

I loved to eat and loved to drink. For me it wasn't uncommon to get together with my friend Marshall and spend the day barbecuing and drinking. We'd barbecue like a brisket and chicken and something else and start with a 12-pack of beer on ice and then go out for more beer. We'd eat and drink all day and all night. That was common. I never thought it was a problem then but I was an alcoholic. There were a lot of times I can remember blacking out and not knowing what happened. Nothing bad ever happened but I was an alcoholic.

I also used to have a short fuse with people, especially on the road. In Houston, traffic's bad and people are always cutting you off on the road. Everyday, it happens. I'm the kind of guy that wouldn't just let that go. If someone cut me off I'd curse them and call them names or tail-gate 'em and made sure they knew about it. One time, my friend Marshall was following me and saw a guy cut me off and he pulled up in front of me because he knew what I was like and he didn't want anything to happen.

Once I started doing the Qigong all that started to change. I wasn't looking for it. I didn't even want it to change but it did. I hadn't even planned to learn the Qigong.

I took a double major in college and have degrees in chemistry and philosophy. After college I decided I wanted to go into the health field but I knew I didn't want to become a western doctor.

When I was little I went to see an Herbalist/Acupuncturist who really helped me a lot with my severe asthma. So I was already familiar with it and decided to go back to school and study oriental medicine.

One of the courses the college requires is in Qigong. I started taking the class and then some friends told me about Master Chunyi Lin and Spring Forest Qigong and I decided to go to Minneapolis and take one of his classes.

Almost immediately, within a few months, things started to change. One day I had about nine beers on an empty stomach and a couple of shots of whiskey while watching a movie over the course of about three hours and I got sick. For normal people everyone would say that sound's normal. Drink that much on an empty stomach and you get sick. But, for me, that wasn't normal.

When the friend I was with called my friend Marshall and told him what happened, Marshall said something's wrong there. Either he drank a lot more than you think or something's wrong because Ho Jun can drink a lot more than that and he never gets sick. And Marshall's been my

204

friend since high school when I'd drink every day. And, then in college, I was in fraternities and stuff and I would power drink.

Then, a couple months later, Marshall and I went to a Super Bowl party and I had like five beers and was eating food and I got sick. That's when he and I both knew something was definitely, definitely wrong.

And, after that incident, I just couldn't drink. I would drink maybe one beer and I would feel sick. And, I really do like to have wine with my dinner or a couple beers and I can't do that anymore. That's the biggest change. But, everything has changed.

Everything that I used to do to excess, eat meat, eat hot food, use lots of salt, I can't do anymore. Now I don't salt anything and I can't eat hot foods either or meat. I can eat a little bit but there's just no desire for that stuff anymore. My body just won't accept it. All the vegetables and things I used to hate, now, let me tell you, vegetables taste really good and I eat lots of vegetables.

The way I react to things has changed, too. Over time it's all changed. Looking back on it I realize it's been a progression. At first, I'd be driving along and somebody would cut me off and I would still call them a name but I wouldn't make as big a deal about it. Then, as time went on, someone would cut me off and instead of shouting at them I'd say "Well, maybe they didn't see me," when I knew they did. Then, it became, "Well, I hope they don't get in an accident." And, then, instead of getting upset, I'd send them a blessing and say to myself, "I hope they get where they're going safely."

So, over time, studying the Qigong, I've gone from getting totally irate to now I'm shooting them some good energy and love, kindness and forgiveness and wishing

205

them well. I'm just much calmer now.

Those are just some of the obvious things that have happened and started happening almost immediately. Now, it's been over two years and my whole personality has changed. My whole life has changed.

I've come from alcoholism to, like Master Lin says, self-enlightenment. And, don't get me wrong, I'm not saying I'm self-enlightened, but I know I am a much better person now. And, I wasn't looking to do this.

I was not looking for self-enlightenment. I was not looking to change my character. I was not looking to quit drinking. I was not looking to quit eating fatty foods. I was not looking for any of that. All of that was just kind of thrust upon me by doing the Qigong. The more Qigong I did the more I changed.

What I know now is that by doing the Qigong, once you start doing this, you just naturally have to become a better person. You just can't do Qigong healing on people with a bad heart or thinking bad thoughts. It just doesn't work. The Qigong won't work.

Because of that as I started doing more and more Qigong I just became a better and better person. It just came as kind of a by-product. Now, I think it's great. I love it. I think everyone should do Qigong.

It's like Master Chunyi Lin says Level One Spring Forest Qigong is kind of like self-help, Level Two is about helping others to heal, Level Three is about self-enlightenment, and Level Four is about enlightening others. And, it takes time. It happens over time and over time it just clicks and keeps clicking.

I have a better understanding now of how everyone is special. I realize that I am special and so is every other person and we should all be treated with the same love and respect. It's like the old saying, the Golden Rule, "Do unto others as you would have them do unto you." That's just the way it is.

I've incorporated the Qigong into my acupuncture and I've used just the Spring Forest Qigong to help lots of people. And it works. I've helped people with all kinds of things. I've helped my friend Marshall's mother with arthritis. It works really well with everything from simple aches and pains, to irritable bowel syndrome and lumps and all kinds of things. It has worked on virtually everyone I've ever used it with.

The Qigong I learned at school is kind of like Level One Spring Forest Qigong but that's all. That's why I've continued to study and will continue to study with Master Chunyi Lin. He's so open and willing to share his knowledge and in my experience that's kind of rare in the field.

Most of the other Qigong people I know kind of want to keep it to themselves, but not him. He's just the opposite. He wants to share what he knows and says everybody can do this and they can. I hope they will. I think everybody should do it.

COLLEAYN T. KLAIBOURNE
Red Wing, MN

Severe Allergic Reactions

In 1991, a week after graduating from college, I had a near death experience due to an allergic food reaction that changed my life forever. It has been a journey from that point on trying to get better and regain health.

I had moved from Minnesota to Colorado to do an internship and my parents and I had spent our last day together in the mountains where I had the severe reaction. I was an hour away from help, but by the time we reached my new home, I was regaining consciousness. Right from that moment I changed. I was going into interior architecture/ space planning before this happened and the next morning I knew I had to pursue the healing and spiritual arts.

This experience made my connection to the spiritual world so much more meaningful than ever before. Words cannot express the feelings experienced during the time I was with the angels. One minute I was experiencing pain and the effects of an allergic reaction; the next I was in the Light. I was in a place of complete, unconditional and powerful love like I had never felt before. Something very powerful happened to me in Spirit. I found a beautiful and radiant life in this Light and that there is only love and complete acceptance for all.

I have worked with my inner self for 11 years and have learned different ancient wisdom teachings, meditation techniques and healing modalities such as Healing Touch, Reiki, Flower Essence work, etc. I attended 4 years at Sancta Sophia Seminary as part of the drive I needed to pursue at that time.

Despite all that I was learning and practicing, I continued to go through swings of poor health, feeling a bit better and again falling back down again. The final low point in my health, a couple of years ago, I began praying for the right person who could help me since my doctors did not have the answers either. Two weeks later I met Chunyi Lin and I am so grateful for his presence in my life.

When I began learning Spring Forest Qigong I knew that this is what I was searching for. Within a few weeks of practicing Qigong twice a day I was seeing positive results. I went from 5 years of being nearly flat on my back, weighing 85 pounds, and experiencing debilitating symptoms to regaining energy and some strength to move around. Other people couldn't believe the changes in my progress and my neurologist at Mayo Clinic has recently asked what I am doing to help myself. This Doctor is unable to help many of his patients get to the point where I am now and I can't wait to show him continuing progress as I beat more odds.

I use Spring Forest Qigong with a client base. People are drawn to me from my own experiences and comment on the peace and calmness that I have within me. They want to do whatever it is that I am doing to help myself. Individuals come for different reasons, some to reduce stress, to feel connected with Spirit, to help them on their own path when they feel so much inner struggle and for health and wellness.

One amazing story happened in the summer of 2001. A woman, whom I have worked with in the past, came to me because she was under a lot of stress. She did not tell me that her father was dying. When I was working with her, I detected huge blocks in her lungs that were not normal for her. I had never felt something so thick, heavy and dense. I removed blockages wherever I was guided to do even though I thought it was so unusual. I do not usually tell people what blockages I work with and I keep in mind that Chunyi Lin tells us to reinforce and keep the experience positive to not bring up any fears. Something kept tugging at me to share the blockages that I detected with her. I said, "I don't know if you are working around toxins, chemicals or smokers, but just be aware of what you're breathing because dense blockages were detected in your lungs". Intuitively I let her know that I felt as though I was working on her father. She then told me that her father was dying of emphysema and lung cancer complicated with pneumonia. Her father lived 7 hours away and she was on her way to be with him because he wasn't expected to survive the night. She felt that she needed to balance her system before she left town.

A few days later she called me and said, "You're not going to believe it!" When she got to the hospital her father was conscious, laughing and telling jokes. The doctors couldn't figure out how his condition had changed so drastically and discharged him. He unexpectedly survived another 6 months.

This client came to me to help her through a difficult time and it was as if a force higher than her had brought her in to help her father. For me it taught me that you don't even need to know what is going on with the person and that miracles can happen at any distance. You just use the skills that you know to help people with pure love, kindness and forgiveness and whatever needs to be worked on will happen. It's like Chunyi Lin says, just work on the blocks and let the outcome happen. It's a power bigger than us.

I used to think that God, the Angels, our Masters…were somewhere in the clouds, way far away. Now I know that they are only a breath away. Whenever I do Qigong for myself or for others, it is my time to reconnect with the same Light and love that I experienced during my near death experience. I am happy to share this feeling of the Light through Qigong and know that anyone can connect with this same energy. The quiet time during Qigong meditation is time to connect with Spirit, our loved ones and ourselves.

STACY LANGAGER
Rockford, MN

Fibrocystic Breast Disease, Migraines, Allergies& Helping Others

In 1999, Master Lin asked me to give my testimonial on how Qigong had changed my life. My story was printed in an advertisement and mailed to hundreds of people. My address was included in the ad for those who may have had questions or concerns.

The response was amazing. I received letters and phone calls from many people across the country. Some of their inquiries and health problems included;

- A man from Chicago, IL with arthritis, very poor vision and stomach ulcers
- A man from Redondo Beach, CA who was a long time allergy sufferer
- . A man from Berwin, IL with an enlarged prostate
- A man from Stockton, CA with allergies and many old sports injuries
- A woman from Lansing, MI with multiple breast lumps
- A woman from Colorado who was curious as to how Qigong could enhance her healthy life
- A man from Mineral Point, MO who wants to study the effects of Qigong on people in prison, juvenile detention centers and psychiatric facilities
- A woman from Chetek, WI with a hyperactive thyroid
- A man from Seattle, WA with severe back pain, his wife with chronic allergies
- A boy from Rockford, MN with croup - swelling of the airway due to allergies. His sister with motion sickness.

I know at least 10 people listed above have been helped through Qigong.

The woman from Chetek, WI is my mother. She went to her doctor in October of 2000. She needed a physical and had been struggling with weight loss.

Her doctor performed a thyroid function test. The results came back abnormal. Her thyroid was not functioning correctly. The doctor's findings were:

T3 elevated to 204 ng/dl (normal range 80 - 180)
T4 elevated to 117 ng/dl (normal range 0.71 to 1.85)
TSH below normal at 0.03 (normal range 0.3 to 5.0)

The doctor's diagnosis was hyperthyroidism with border line T3 toxicosis. The doctor's report stated this could lead to Grave's disease or Hashimoto's thyroiditis.

My mother's doctor tested her thyroid again in November of 2000. Her T3 increased even more to 250 ng/dl. This scared my mom. Her doctor offered no cure, only radiation and medication to control her thyroid. She would need the medication for the rest of her life.

In December 2000, after my level III Spring Forest Qigong retreat, my mother came to me. She informed me about her thyroid problem and most definitely did not want to go through radiation. She asked me to give her a Qigong treatment. I was so happy she came to me for help.

I gave her a Qigong treatment. For a few seconds during the treatment, it was hard for her to catch her breath. She said it felt like something had left her body. After the treatment, she felt different; very relaxed and like her illness was gone.

In May 2001, my mother returned to her doctor for another thyroid function test. Amazingly, the results came back NORMAL! Her T3 was 163 ng/dl (normal range is 80 - 180). This was after one and only one Qigong treatment.

My mother practices Spring Forest Qigong on a weekly basis. She says the healing and calming effects of Qigong are wonderful!

The two children from Rockford, MN are mine. My son was rushed to the Emergency Room twice because he couldn't breathe. He had severe allergies to dust and mold. He was put on steroids to control the swelling in his airway. The steroids made him more susceptible to other illness. He missed 30 days of kindergarten. He was a sick little boy!

After practicing Spring Forest Qigong, he has not had a reoccurrence with croup for three years. He says Qigong makes him feel better inside, makes it easier for him to breathe and calms him down. He is healthy now. He missed three days of school last year.

My daughter struggled with motion sickness for over a year. We tried everything we could to help her; oral medication, elastic bands around her wrists and stickers behind her ears. Nothing worked for her.

Through Qigong, she has not had motion sickness for almost three years. She knows how to clear the blockage in her forehead that causes the motion sickness. Doing Qigong makes her forehead and stomach feel better. She says she can feel the blockage leave her body and then she doesn't feel sick anymore.

Now to update my story. I don't have any breast lumps! No more migraines! I am allergy free! I am completely healed and I feel great!

When I participated in the video testimonial in 1999, I was four months pregnant. Qigong helped quell my morning sickness. My labor from the first contraction until I was holding my baby in my arms was only three hours. I didn't need any pain medication either!

I saw Master Lin when I was five months pregnant. I asked him if he could tell me the sex of my baby. He waved his hand over my belly and said it would be a boy. He was right!

My husband and I have completed three levels of Spring Forest Qigong classes. We practice Qigong on a daily basis as a family, children included. Qigong is a journey where you are physically, emotionally and spiritually healed. The power of Qigong is amazing!

LOUISE LUDFORD
Minneapolis, MN

Disabling Panic, Anxiety Attacks

October of 1986 I was working in a school when suddenly I couldn't breathe, my heart started racing, I was dizzy and perspiring, my body trembling uncontrollably. I thought I was dying.

A student guided me to the nurse's office and from there I was transported by ambulance to the hospital. The diagnosis was panic attack. But, the symptoms worsened.

At one point, I started stuttering, developed migraines and the left side of my body became numb. Walking was difficult, I lost my relationship to the ground below me. Fear and terror gripped my mind and body. I lost all confidence and trust in myself and the world around me. For the next eleven years panic and anxiety attacks took over my life.

I believed the doctors had misdiagnosed my illness. I thought there was something wrong with my heart but all the tests indicated my heart was functioning just fine. My heart as a physical organ was working perfectly. However, my heart as a soul-spiritual organ was weak. The heart's nourishing forces of love, hope, joy, faith and courage were not warming nor vitalizing my body. My heart, my sun, had been eclipsed by fear. I was in desperate need of help.

About seven years after my first panic attack, I started hearing about the practice and teaching of Qigong meditation in China. I immediately knew this was a study I wanted to pursue. However, living in a state of panic and anxiety twenty-four hours a day, a trip to China was not an option. I could feel a sense of urgency to meditate. In

216

my heart and mind I knew there was a teacher out there who would help me and teach me to meditate but I had no idea who he was or how to find him.

Some time later, my parents showed me a newspaper article featuring a man who was teaching Qigong in the Twin Cities. As I looked at the picture of the instructor and his students my eyes were pulled to the instructor, and I remember thinking, "Oh, there you are, but this doesn't look like you." My eyes scanned the article but again they were pulled right back to the man standing in front of the students. And I stood there staring at the newspaper photo. After awhile I wondered why I was still standing there staring at the man. Then, sadness came over me, for I wanted to study Qigong but I didn't have the strength to drive myself to a class.

August of 1997, I was in the middle of a panic attack sitting on the couch in my parent's living room. I was flipping through the cable stations and caught the last two minutes of a community cable program. Chunyi Lin was being interviewed. When I saw him I literally jumped off the couch with joy and exclaimed, "There you are! You are my teacher and you are going to teach me everything I need to know!"

The interviewer asked him one last question which was , "Can you leave our viewers with something they can practice at home?" Master Lin showed the hand and breathing movements of the Seven Steps of New Life. I followed along and it had an immediate effect on me. The program ended. I quickly wrote down the telephone number, called for a catalog and signed up for Levels I, II, & III and two Tai Chi classes.

Level I began in October at Anoka-Ramsey Community College. It was quite far away from my home for my comfort level, but I was bound and determined to attend this class. I made it to the college, but the parking lot was full. I did not have the strength to walk from the parking lot down the hill then back up to the building so I parked illegally and went to class. I felt so dizzy and faint I thought I would have to crawl in. I made it. The only seat available was in the front center. And, all I could say at this point was "Let the healings begin...."

While sitting in class I noticed that whenever Master Lin stood in front of me I felt strong, I could sit upright. When he walked to the other side of the room I felt weak, sick and faint. Well, he walked back and forth standing in front of me lecturing and then moving to the other side before I figured out that I felt stronger and healthier when he stood before me. Then he moved away again and as I felt my body slump down to the table, in my mind, I asked him, "Please come over and stand by me." No, my mental request was not that polite. It was more like, "Oh my God, get over here!" He did so and stood in front of me the remainder of the class. Smiling at me and staring right into my heart.

That evening I realized I found something very special, a form of meditation and a teacher who opens his heart to his students. He is like a godparent, who watches over one's soul yet honors the individual freedom of each student to walk their own path of meditation and discovery. His style of teaching is gentle, the source of his teaching is love.

When I signed up for Spring Forest Qigong, I had no idea that Master Lin was a healer and that in addition to teaching us how to meditate, he would be teaching us how to heal ourselves and how to help others to heal. To give and receive is an example that flows from nature.

You can see it in the water cycle through evaporation and precipitation; in our relationship to the plant kingdom with the exchange of carbon dioxide and oxygen. We are truly in a relationship with everything around us. Master Lin teaches us as we receive this universal love, to remember to return this love to the universe, and to people through actions of good deeds, kindness, love and forgiveness.

I have been practicing Spring Forest Qigong ever since that first class. The meditations have been my daily bread, and the medicine my heart needed to heal. I thought I had been living in a total eclipse of my heart, but perhaps there was one stream of light that refused to be eclipsed by fear. If I could name that beam of light it would be hope. Hope gave me the strength to search for the healing medicine my heart so desperately needed. The medicine is love. It does conquer all.

Through the practice of Spring Forest Qigong meditation, panic and anxiety have shifted away and in their place I feel the rays of love, peace, hope and faith stream outward. As the physical sun gives healing rays of light, warmth, and life to the earth, I will continue to strive to keep the channels of my heart open in order to serve and breathe back to the universe the healing rays of love, peace, hope and faith.

Master Lin, with deep gratitude, thank you for your teachings, your healings and your love.

ANGIE MEIERDING
Burnsville, MN

Long Distance Healing

I was born and raised on a farm near Clements, MN. For as long as I can remember I have been interested in alternative healing and the spiritual side of life. Friends from Minneapolis told us about this Chinese man at Anoka-Ramsey College who did some sort of Chinese healing. My husband, Joseph, and I contacted the college and attended an informational evening introducing Master Lin and Qigong. We were intrigued and decided to sign up for Qigong classes. We were getting ready to move to Texas and wanted to complete Level 1 & Level 2 before the move.

The classes were most interesting. As I listened to what Master Lin had to say there was logic and reason in the concept of Qigong. Why shouldn't we be able as creatures of God to use universal energy to heal others and ourselves? Why not acknowledge and utilize the energy within? It made logical, reasonable sense to me. What Master Lin teaches makes sense to me therefore, for me it is true.

My husband and I both try to be very proactive about our health. We exercise and take nutritional supplements. Initially, my pro-active approach to health stemmed from my having some problems with western medicine. I am terribly allergic to antibiotics and most prescription drugs. Taking medication often prolonged my recovery. Some years ago, I had what was referred to as a simple operation to remove veins in my legs. I was supposed to be in-and-out of day surgery in a couple of hours. But, I went from the operating room to the coronary unit. My husband thought he was going to lose me. And, it was all because I was allergic to the anesthetic. The antibiotics and pain prescriptions also reacted negatively to my system and I was taking additional drugs to counter-act the negative side effects of the first round of drugs. Several weeks were added to my recovery time.

Experiences like this one and several others over my lifetime have prompted me to ask what can I do for myself to avoid getting into trouble again? I just knew in the core of my being that what Master Lin said was true and Spring Forest Qigong would work for me. We completed the classes and moved to Texas in the fall of 1998.

It was in Texas that I had my incident with the spider and experienced long-distance Qigong healing. The workspace at my new office had not been used for some time. It had old supplies stacked on the floor and the area needed to be cleaned-up before I could feel comfortable working.

I got down on the floor and was going through a pile of brochures stacked under a desk. When I got to the bottom of the stack a small spider about the size of a wood tick, but with long, odd-looking legs (like extra big wheels on a truck) came right at me – very fast – like a racing spider. He was speeding right toward my knees and without thinking I smashed him with my right hand. He "died" about four o'clock in the afternoon. As I was driving home I noticed I had a bump on my middle finger about the size of a pea. It was painful and felt stiff. I thought that little spider must have bit me.

I came home and told Joseph what happened and explained that my finger and hand was feeling kind of weird. In the morning, my hand was swollen and Joseph said maybe I should call the doctor. But, I didn't want to

221

do that because of my past experience with western medicine and drugs. I didn't want to risk making the incident worse. After all, it was such a little spider. I thought it would turn out like a bee sting and be okay in a day or two.

By the time I came home from work that night the swelling and stiffness was up past my elbow and tender under my arm. Joseph told me I was starting to act a little goofy. He called Master Lin and handed the phone to me. I told Master Lin I had been bitten by a little black spider. Master Lin said, "No, it was a brown spider." And then I realized he was right, it was a brown spider. Little did I know until about a year later that it is known as a brown recluse spider and it is very poisonous. Their favorite places to hide are under and behind undisturbed stacks of boxes and junk.

Master Lin advised me that I might have to incorporate western medicine along with the Qigong because the poison had spread and the brown spider is extremely poisonous. I said no. I'm confidant Qigong will work for me. I was more concerned about what western drugs would do to me.

Master Lin instructed me to fill a glass of water and place my hand over the glass. Next, I was to drink some of the water and replace my hand over the glass. Master Lin sent long-distance Qigong healing energy to me. After the healing I followed Master Lin's instruction and sat quietly for 15 minutes. Next I did the Small Universe meditation. I went to bed and when I got up in the morning, the swelling underneath my arm was gone. The swelling started at my finger and ended at my elbow. I was so grateful for the healing and felt confident that I had taken the right course of action.

I went to work that day and since Master Lin had said to call him again I called that evening as well. We went through the same routine as the night before. I followed with the Small Universe meditation after sitting quietly for 15 minutes. In the morning, the swelling had receded to just my hand and fingers.

I called Master Lin the third night, and received my third long-distance healing. Master Lin said it would take ten days or so for my condition to clear up. And he was right. The next morning, the swelling was gone and I was back to a pea sized bump on my finger, which vanished in approximately 10-14 days.

About a year later, I was talking to a woman from Texas who is a BSRN and teaches at one of the nurses' colleges. We were discussing alternative medicine and how the curriculum at her school has changed over the years and now included classes dealing with alternative concepts. I told her about the spider bite and that's when I discovered it was most likely a brown recluse spider that bit me. She relayed several incidents of students coming from the North and not being aware of poisonous spiders. They too, did not give much thought to being bit and thought it would pass in a day or two. Both of the people she told me about ended up in the hospital near death.

I am grateful to Master Lin for sending Qigong healing over the telephone to me. And for our being able to attend Qigong classes.

I've had several other healing experiences with Master Lin and Spring Forest Qigong. The most recent one was in March 2001. We had returned to Minnesota and it was the last day of a big ice storm. I went into the office early and had to go around to the side of the building to get in. I slipped on the ice and my legs flew out from under me

223

and I came crashing down on my elbow. I went home wearing a sling and instructed not to drive for four to six weeks. I am in sales and I live in my car. I had to do something fast.

The next day we went to see Master Lin and I had my arm in the sling and was hobbling around due to bumps and bruises on my body. I couldn't rotate or lift up my arm. Master Lin treated me with Qigong and when he was done he said take your sling off. So, I took my sling off and he said rotate your arm and I said "Ooo-kay." I was amazed. I could rotate and lift my arm. Master Lin cleared the blockages away from the injury and there I was the very next day using my arm without any pain.

It is just amazing and wonderful how Master Lin uses Spring Forest Qigong. He could keep the knowledge to himself but he believes in sharing and teaching others to do what he does. Master Lin shares his gift with anyone who asks for healing and who is open to exploring new ways of thinking. For me, Spring Forest Qigong is the best gift I have ever received. I believe Spring Forest Qigong and Master Lin saved me much pain and suffering and possibly saved my life. Having Spring Forest Qigong in my medicine cabinet and Master Lin as my teacher I am prepared to enjoy my life to the fullest.

CRES SCHRAMM
Ramsey, MN

A Skeptic's Experience

I have taken Master Lin's Level I through IV of Spring Forest Qigong at Anoka-Ramsey Community College. I began Level I in June of 2001 and completed Level IV in February of 2002. The reason I took Spring Forest Qigong is because I know many people who are in pain or who have illnesses and I wanted to be able to try to help them instead of feeling so helpless. I have had many positive experiences from the very first class with Spring Forest Qigong, but I can honestly tell you that how I came to this class and how I came to believe in qigong is another story.

My mother-in-law, Bernice, had been going to some sort of healer, possibly Reiki, for quite some time. Our family believed that this was a bunch of "malarkey" but she continued to go anyway, claiming she felt better after each treatment.

Bernice had a severe stroke in December of 1998 during the holidays. She had been living independently up to this point. She celebrated her 81st birthday in February of 1999 in a nursing home, and after nearly three months of rehabilitation, we knew she could not live alone anymore. She had lost much use of her right side. Bernice came to live in our home with my husband, children and I in March of 1999. I spent many hours taking her to physical and occupational therapy, and by the end of the summer she was out of her wheel chair and using a quad-cane and walker. Her speech was getting better, but never returned to its normal pattern.

Even for all of the accomplishment Bernice had made

225

and all the encouragement we gave, she was never happy or accepting of what had happened to her. We told her that some of her peers were not doing as well as she was, and they hadn't even had a stroke. Still, she had a difficult time with her successes, because they weren't enough to get her back to her former health.

Throughout this period of time, there was a group of people she had maintained in contact with—people whom she met through the healer she went to prior to her stroke. In August of 2000, one of her friends called to tell her that the healer had died, but she heard of another one.

Mom asked me to get on the phone and take down the number. I rolled my eyes, but complied. The number was for Chunyi Lin in Andover. After I hung up, I thought..."I know who this is." Chunyi is a friend of a fellow who goes to our parish...Don Omundson. Chunyi had been to our parish before, but I didn't know he did this healing stuff.

I thought to myself, "Well, at least I know someone who knows him and I can check this out," feeling a little less apprehensive about who I might be dealing with. I had been warned about "quacks" all my life. I know Don, from our parish, pretty well and he is an honorable man, so I felt he wouldn't be hanging out with a phony. Through Don I found out it was called Qigong.

I made the appointment with Chunyi for the middle of September. By this time he had moved to Chanhassen. Of course, this was now at the other end of the earth to me, since we reside in Ramsey, near Anoka.

The day came and I was hoping this would help, but I also dreaded driving to Chanhassen, maneuvering an elderly woman who could barely walk.

Chunyi had about six people waiting for his help. He

was kind and polite to all of them. I knew how busy he was, and how he must seem like the last hope to many. Even when I made the appointment back in August, I knew that he must be very busy and that he was squeezing us in out of kindness.

As he led Bernice and I to a living room area, I wondered what to expect since I had never seen this done before. We talked a bit about what happened to Bernice and then he started doing this weird thing with his fingers. From my angle it looked crazy and I thought...this is not going to work. He told that me if I would have brought Bernice to him soon after the stroke, he would have been able to help her more, but that it would take her a few more treatments. "Well," I thought, "at $60 per treatment and almost 50 miles one way, I don't see this happening." We thanked him and left and joked about it on the way home, figuring, well that was worth it-ha-ha.

I told a friend of mine, Shelli Pittman, about my experience. She said, "You know Elizabeth (from our parish) took a class on that. Remember when I had the pain in my tooth area that was so bad I was on three Tylenol codeines every 3-4 hours? I had gone to the doctor and the dentist and neither could find anything wrong. Well, Elizabeth took me into the Sanctuary after church one Sunday and did this deal that whisked away the pain." "Really?" I asked. "HMMMM," I thought.

Time passed and Mom, as far as she could articulate, never felt better. But when I received the ARCC mailing in January of 2001 for classes for Spring/Summer of 2001, I noticed that Qigong was being offered. I made a mental note of the date and set the course catalog aside. Periodically through early spring, I would come across it again, make another mental note of the Qigong and toss it aside. When the end of May came, I stumbled across it again, under a pile of magazines, and began to give it serious thought.

I was having a conflict with the eastern philosophy versus Christian belief. I didn't want to take something that would have me compromise my strong Christian faith, and I also didn't want to jeopardize my spirit by opening myself up to something that may be harmful to my soul and being.

I began to pray intensely about this because somehow this was being presented to me and I was being drawn to do this. In my daily life, I listen strongly to the voice within me who I believe to be the Holy Spirit, so I didn't want to ignore this persistent thought, yet I didn't want to be lured by something else.

I called the Friday before the class was to begin and asked if there was room for enrollment. Yes, there was. I didn't enroll. I prayed to God that if I were to go to this class, it would happen and if not, He would put the obstacles up to not allow this if this was not His will. I continued to pray.

On Tuesday before class, I dropped by ARCC. I figured I should at least give the instructor a little notice. Was there still space available? Yes. I enrolled, believing that this would come to a screeching halt, as other things in my life had, if this was not to occur. Obviously, I was supposed to be there, since I attended all of the three-day conference for Level I & II.

I wondered, when I talked with Chunyi at class, if he remembered me. I'm sure he could sense how skeptical I was when I first brought my mother-in-law back in September. As I took his classes, I felt energy surges in my hands and body that I figured I would not be able to experience, and as he passed us in class I could feel the healing energy he was using to help each of us with our individual problems. I now believe that I had been feeling these tingling sensations before I knew of Qigong, but I thought my feet were going to fall asleep, or some other strange reason. I had also kept my husband quite busy changing light bulbs around our home because they seemed to "pop" when I would turn on the switches or walk by them. I even told my husband jokingly that I must have an electrifying personality.

Chunyi challenged us to begin using our technique right away. On Saturday, June 2, 2001, in the evening after my first class in Level II, I asked my daughter if she had any problems. Her knees were bothering her again. She was 16 and had been dancing since she was 4. This was the first year she had not danced and it was difficult for her to make that decision because she loved it, but she decided it was best to give it up because her knees hurt so bad and she was on Relefen, a painkiller.

I used Sword Fingers and worked on her knees. She noticed immediate relief. Her knees have not bothered her since that time, except when we moved her aunt from one home to another where there was a lot of hard work involved. Any pain she experiences now after something strenuous is very low key, if any, and is nothing like the pain before I treated her. When she has a flare-up, she asks me to Qigong her.

One of the most amazing experiences that happened to me occurred June 11, 2001 after I completed my Level II. A friend of mine, Shelli Pittman, brought her mother and sister, who were visiting from South Carolina, to my place so I could "ear cone" or candle their ears to remove the wax buildup. While I was doing this we talked. Shelli mentioned how her mom's hips were so sore all of the time and that she probably would end up having hip surgery. She could hardly walk because of the pain.

We talked of other things while I finished their ear coning and then they were ready to leave. As we stood in my dining room, I casually asked Yvonne, her mother, if she would like me to try to Qigong her. I told her I just finished the class and I wasn't sure if it would help. She said "ok."

I just did the basic Sword Fingers and didn't put her in the small universe. I opened the blockages in her hips and began to remove the energy. She stood there making faces, and I thought, "She's thinking I'm a goof." When I was through, I said..."Yah, you'll go back to South Carolina and tell your friends about Shelli's weird friend who does ear coning and Qigong." We all laughed.

The next morning, my phone rang at 8:30 a.m. It was Shelli. She asked if I was going to be in her area at all that day. I told her I had some errands. "Why?" I asked. She told me that when they left my house the previous evening, her mother got right up into the mini-van with no problem...she got out of the mini-van and walked up the stairs to Shelli's home without flinching. Shelli had asked her mother, "Mom, are you ok, do you feel anything?" Yvonne said, "I'm fine."

Shelli wanted to know if I could stop over to give her mom another treatment before their flight back to South Carolina at 1:30 p.m. that day. I agreed to be there at 10:00 a.m. When I arrived, Shelli's sister said, "Cres, you know I've slept in the same room as my mother before, and she's never slept through the whole night. She is in so much pain that she groans because the pain burns in her hips. Last night she didn't even wake up and she made no sound."

Just then, her mother walked up twelve steps from the basement with a bounce. She said, "There's the woman who healed me!" I was embarrassed and amazed. This time, I put her in the small universe, and worked on her spine, hips, and feet. When I was through, she thanked me and said, "You made a believer out of me."

Shelli explained to me, also, that her mom was making those weird faces because she could feel something being pulled from her hips the night before, and it felt strange. Since that treatment June 11, I have continued to ask Shelli about her mom's pain. Her mother has no pain and walks without a problem. In August, when Shelli went to visit, her mom was fine and just beginning to feel a tiny bit of discomfort. I told Shelli I would be learning some long-distance healing soon.

I have done Qigong on my husband for acid reflux/hiatus hernia, and while he won't admit it, his symptoms of gagging have not been as frequent. One night I had finished doing my Qigong exercises after he had gone to bed. This was around 12:00 a.m. and I could really feel the energy. I decided I would Qigong him while he was sleeping, because he is a worse skeptic than I am, so I quietly crept into our bedroom. I stood there in the dark, waving my arms around him, opening blockages and removing, saying to myself, "Blockages open, acid reflux gone, completely healed," and worked to removed blockages in his whole body.

I thought to myself how I must look, and wondered what would he think if he woke up. During this whole time, however, he continued to sleep—and snore loudly. I waved my hands over him and said, blockages open, snoring gone, completely healed—-he stopped right then and there. Not one peep. In fact, he was very quiet in his breathing. I finished up and left the room and told my 19-year old daughter that I just Qigonged Dad and that he stopped snoring on the spot. We laughed. But when I went to bed a half-hour later, I was almost worried because he was breathing so quietly I had to make sure he was still breathing. He was and he continued sleeping softly for the rest of the evening.

I have used Qigong on my pets. Recently our beagle, Josie, had signs of tonsillitis again. She gets it from eating things she shouldn't. I decided to try Qigong on her before taking her to the vet. Her symptoms were gone by the next morning.

Prior to Christmas of 2001, my daughter noticed her Beta fish was not looking good. When she mentioned this to me, I told her I would be happy to Qigong it. She decided to keep that in mind but a few days later, her fish was on its side. She carried the small tank with the fish to the kitchen and asked me to Qigong it. I looked at the fish and thought, this isn't going to work...he's almost a goner. I put the whole tank in the small universe, and worked on the fish. A few days later, my daughter thanked me for helping her fish get better. The fish was healthy and lived for another seven months.

The same thing happened with my niece's Oscar fish. At Christmas, I was upstairs visiting at my sister's house when one of my teenaged nieces came upstairs and summoned me to come to the lower level. I was told that the Oscar had apparently jumped out of the large aquarium and had been out of water for an uncertain amount of time, on the floor behind the tank. They had returned the fish to the aquarium, where it was on its side at the bottom of the tank, lifeless. Again, I thought to myself,

"Good luck, fish." I used Sword Fingers to send energy and remove blockages. It moved a little. I finished up and went upstairs, shaking my head. Needless to say, the fish survived and is still alive.

In January of 2002, I fell and severely sprained my ankle. It hurt so bad, I could hardly drive. I had heard it snap when I fell forward and to the side and thought I may have broken it. When I got home and as my husband drove me to Urgent Care, I began sending energy to my ankle. I continued doing so in the waiting room as I waited to see a doctor. The pain lessened as I waited.

When I saw the doctor, he told me it was a bad sprain and gave me a gel-cast ankle brace to wear for six weeks. He was very emphatic and stern about wearing the brace. For the first week, my ankle hurt so bad that I was cussing every time I had to put my tennis shoe on over the brace because it would bend my Achilles tendon. A couple of nurses I know said I might have been better off breaking it. I had continued doing Qigong and by the end of the second week, my ankle was feeling much better. After week three I was able to walk without limping and only wore the brace if I was going to be doing stressful work like going up and down ladders while I was wallpapering or for excessive walking.

Up until this point, I had only experienced Qigong through classes, by doing my own Qigong exercises for my personal health or by actually doing Qigong to help other people. I knew that I had been healthier than ever. Normally each fall, I would get a cold and sinus infection that would last for a couple of months, and I would usually be on antibiotics for two prescription refills. This past winter I would do my Qigong exercises, and any symptom I had, either cold or flu, would disappear within a day. But I never actually had someone Qigong me.

In June of 2002 I was going to have a hysterectomy and I was very frightened of the impending surgery. It was the first time I was going to be in the hospital since I had my youngest child seventeen years ago, with the exception of a short-stay day surgery a few years back. This was going to be major surgery, and although I trusted God to keep me safe, and knew I had many people praying for me, I couldn't help feeling uneasy. I wanted to do what I could to prepare my body for surgery.

I continued my Qigong exercises to remove blockages so that I would heal faster from my surgery. While I felt I would be able to remove a lot of blockages, I didn't want to take any chances. I wanted to call in the "big guns", so I asked Jim, Chunyi's associate, to Qigong me. I told Jim I thought of him as "The Drano Guy"...that he would be able to get rid of anything I wouldn't be able to.

Jim did Qigong me, told me where he felt blockages and what he worked on. He also reminded me that I might feel pain where the energy was healing before I felt better and although I'm a very positive person, Jim made me feel at ease about my surgery by giving me some advice on how to quell any nerve-wracking thoughts about my outcome. The next day I felt like a truck rolled over me, and then the pain that had been nagging me in certain areas, the areas Jim detected, completely left.

Surgery day, Friday, had arrived and among my personal items I brought was a Walkman and Chunyi's "Self-Concentration/Small Universe" tape. I figured even though I might be tired, hurting and in no mood to do anything, the least I could probably do was just listen to these with no effort.

I had given my daughters strict instructions to contact

Chunyi or Jim if there were any major complications with the surgery. While I didn't really expect any, I was aware that strange accidents have occurred. My surgery, scheduled for 12:30 p.m. was a total hysterectomy with anterior-posterior repair.

When the surgery and recovery was completed, about 4:00 p.m., I was rolled into my hospital room and hooked up to an IV PCA (patient controlled analgesia) pump that contained morphine, which I could control by pressing a button. It would allow me to dispense morphine when I felt discomfort, but not sooner than every fifteen minutes to prevent overdose.

When the nurses would ask me about my level of pain, rated 1-10 with 10 being extreme pain, my level was around 4-5. Later that evening, still a little dazed, but coherent, I listened to my tape. The next morning the nurses remarked at how well I was doing and asked me what my pain level was. I told them 3-4 and by 9:00 a.m. they replaced my PCA pump with ibuprofin and gave me Percicet every 6 hours.

When the pastor from our parish came to visit that afternoon, he couldn't believe I had major surgery because I looked so good. I was feeling pretty good, too. I had curled my hair, put on makeup and taken a couple of walks. I only had some discomfort in my back, but I didn't feel like I had uterine removal and reconstructive repair done. I was expecting to be very sore. Again, when I rested at night, I prayed and gave thanks, then listened to my tape.

On Sunday, I waited to see the doctor. She had done such a good job and was so caring. She told me I would be able to go home that afternoon. My pain level was down to 2-3. I was off the I.V. and only received a Percicet in the morning. The nurses couldn't believe how well I was doing and I was home by 3:00 p.m. My husband had a prescription of Percicet filled and I was told to take ibuprofin after I no longer needed Percicet. I took two Percicets the rest of Sunday and one Percicet on Monday and switched over to ibuprofin completely, only 3 days after major surgery.

Later that week, I heard a good song on the radio and started to be-bop around the kitchen. Quickly I scolded myself. I was supposed to take it easy-no vacuuming, with no lifting of over 10 pounds for six weeks. I felt so good I had to remind myself not to overdo it. I didn't feel like I had major surgery at all, with the exception of a few uncomfortable stitches and some tiredness, but even my energy level was good.

Was it a typical recovery? Maybe...or maybe not, but I think I owe the success of my surgery and my quick, painless recovery to God for keeping me in His care, all the people who prayed for me and for the knowledge and power of Qigong.

I believe strongly in God, in my Christian faith, and in the power of prayer. I have seen many miracles happen and I have seen wonderful healings at Trinity Episcopal Church, but I never believed I would have the chance to help in the process of healing myself, and others with so many positive, quick results.

I offer my help to many, making sure they are aware that it is a higher power using me as a tool to help in their healing. I tell them that they have the capability to do this on their own, and that I can show them some basics...all they need is to be loving, kind, forgiving and to have confidence. Not many are willing to ask me for help or to show them how to help themselves. Many chuckle to themselves as I once did.

There are many things in this world that we cannot explain. I am a skeptic of many things, and probably will continue to be. But I know that since I have taken Spring Forest Qigong, I will not be as skeptical as I once was. I have encouraged those who are chronically sick to look into Spring Forest Qigong to help in their own personal health management and healing process.

Knowing how healthy I have personally been keeps me practicing Qigong. Sometimes I don't feel like doing my exercises. It's clear to see, though, that I now feel like I have more control over the actual health and recovery of my body and it is as important to me as someone trying to keep physically fit, so I need to continue practicing to be able to heal myself and others more quickly.

But, what really keeps me exercising and striving to become a better Qigong practitioner is hope...the hope that I can help someone who is not feeling well and maybe ease their pain. For me, to feel helpless and not be able to do anything is such a sad feeling...but at least now I know I can really try.

SUE SIVULA
Maple Grove, Minnesota

Brain Stem Injury

I was going through a tough time in my life emotionally when things started to go wrong physically. When I turned my head my eyes wouldn't follow. I couldn't focus so I couldn't drive. I also had trouble swallowing and choked on food.

I went to a couple of doctors and was told the cause of my difficulties was a vein bleed on my brain stem. They considered a number of things including surgery to correct the problem.

Just a month or so before this happened my cousin Cindy, who worked at Anoka Ramsey Community College, had told me about Chunyi Lin, who also worked at ARCC. She said he was helping people to be well by using QiGong. I decided to make an appointment to see him and have some energy work done.

I had already made an appointment to get a second medical opinion at the Mayo Clinic in Rochester but was able to schedule visits with Chunyi before hand. I went for three sessions with Master Lin and improved after each. I went again, driving myself this time, and he said the blockage was gone. I said "Well, just give me one more treatment so I'll feel good going to Mayo". He said Okay.

When I went to Mayo my vision was back to normal and I was feeling much better. The doctors did tests to check my reflexes and who knows what else. The neurosurgeon there said there was one little thing he noticed with my eyes but unless you were trained in neurosurgery you wouldn't see it. All my symptoms were gone.

They didn't even order a second MRI.

So back home I went to keep a follow up appointment with the neurosurgeon there. She had done a second MRI and I was to get the results that day. When she came in the room she said "I had to look twice because I looked at your second MRI and couldn't figure out why you were even here. She said she had to go back to the original MRI to see where the problem had been. She asked me to come back once a year for a recheck and I said "But I don't need to come back once a year. I feel wonderful". She said "No, you're right. You don't need to come back.

People ask me how all this is possible. I believe it is possible by moving the energy in your body. Things happen in your life, little daily challenges or bigger challenges that cause stress. If you don't know how to work through them these stresses cause your energy to get stuck and cause symptoms of stress or illness. If you can learn to move your energy yourself or have someone move your energy for you, your energy moves freely again. You let go of those things that are causing physical or emotional discomfort. It just clears things up. It's healing. Not only physically but emotionally and spiritually as well.

To me it's a God send. The practice of QiGong is something everyone can benefit from. Once you have had an experience with QiGong you want to keep it a part of your life.

Chunyi Lin and Spring Forest have had an amazing impact on my life. It's given me a way to live life more fully, happier.

Like I said before, Spring Forest QiGong improves your life physically, emotionally and Spiritually. It helps you begin to know the real person you are, to let go of past anger and pain and let the person that is you shine through. There is no changing my mind, everyone could benefit from this amazing energy work.

CHACONAS SPROLES
Aurora, IL

Discovering My Spiritual Path

I have been on a search for my spiritual path my entire life. I have studied Reiki and was a second degree Reiki student before discovering Spring Forest Qigong. In the past few years, I have discovered my spiritual path which has brought me back to Christianity and led me to focusing on healing and helping others. I am preparing now to go to nursing school.

I first learned of Spring Forest Qigong after my mother was diagnosed with MS four years ago. One of her therapists told me of Master Chunyi Lin and the wonderful healing technique that he teaches.

I went to Master Lin's Level 1 class and his teaching just rang so true to everything that I believe and everything that I am and want to be. It was so very enlightening to me. The way he teaches is also done in such love and such caring. It was so clear and true to me that we all have the healing capabilities within us and that it is God working through us.

Master Lin teaches so clearly that he is not the only one that has this healing ability. He is just trying to awaken us as individuals to what is already out there for us. Some teachers get on the selfish route that "I am the only one" who can do these wonderful things. I don't believe that. I believe as Master Lin teaches that there is a higher power behind it and we are all apart of it.

Since starting to study Spring Forest Qigong, I don't get sick anymore. I just don't get sick. I use to suffer from chronic bladder infections and yeast infections. I don't any longer. I also used to be depressed a lot and that

241

seems to be gone. Physically I've just been really good and emotionally and mentally I've just been really strong ever since. Actually, since I started learning from Master Lin, this is the most I've grown in my entire life span.

Instead of trying to go to somebody else for problems, I now go within. I have two small children and now I use Spring Forest Qigong to work on my children whenever they're sick.

For example, this past winter, my one-year-old son got sick with the flu. After two days it was clear it was a severe strain of flu that wasn't going to pass quickly and build his immune system. It was starting to get worse. It was the really nasty flu, with fever and spewing and vomiting and diarrhea. So, on the third day, when he wasn't getting better I used the Spring Forest Qigong to help his body to heal. That was in the morning and by that night he was totally fine.

And my three-year-old daughter never got the flu at all. I believe that's largely because she would mimic me when I practiced the Active Exercises for Spring Forest Qigong Level 1. She did them along with me and she didn't get sick last winter.

I work on both my children with the Spring Forest Qigong techniques now whenever they get sick. Both of them were born with severe allergies, especially my little boy, and the allergies are pretty much gone now. Whenever he has symptoms coming on, I do the Qigong for him and they just clear up right away. Both of my kids are so healthy now.

To me, Spring Forest Qigong is just so empowering, so simple and yet so powerful. To me, it is the light within you. It's so clear that there is a higher power and it is within all of us and surrounds us and it's just waiting for us to access it. Spring Forest Qigong just takes you right to it. It's got everything. It's got the meditation. It's got the healing aspect. It brings you such a sense of peace and empowerment. It completes you.

SHANNON SWEDBERG
Prior Lake, Minnesota

A Healing Testimony
Cancer Survivor

It is a sincere honor to be able to share my personal story about working with Master Chunyi Lin and my experience with Spring Forest Qigong.

I believe I was led to Master Lin and that it was, at its essence, an answer to prayer and my deepest longing. In the fall of 1998, I was wrestling with some hard decisions. I had just been told that my recent biopsy was positive and that my breast cancer had reoccurred. I had previously had two small lumps removed and followed the standard treatment course - lumpectomy and radiation. I was 34 at the time of my original diagnosis and now, at 38, I was being told that, once again, I had breast cancer.

Cancer had been one of my greatest teachers and I had made many thoughtful decisions about how to take responsibility for my health and my healing. Thinking back on it now, however, I see how "busy" I had been trying to work at maintaining my health. I'm sure many people faced with a cancer diagnosis fall into this pattern...You try to learn as much as you can about cancer, seek out alternative therapies, vitamins, supplements, etc...and attempt to incorporate all this into your life. I had made a clear decision that I was "done" with cancer and was disheartened and discouraged when it returned.

The second time around I knew that I had to approach my healing differently. I had learned many things about the importance of bringing mind, body and spirit together to heal but I don't know how much of it I had actually put into practice. I had a lot of head knowledge and this was actually part of my problem....I also was afraid and I didn't want to make any decisions out of fear.

This is how I was led to Master Lin. I voiced this same concern to a therapist I was seeing at the time. She shared her own experiences working with Master Lin and told me of his wisdom and gifts for healing. She assured me that I could trust his insights. Something resonated deep within when she shared this story and I wanted very much to meet and work with Master Lin.

I will never forget my first session with Master Lin. I felt reverent in his presence...and I still do each time I see him...he is just such a radiant spirit. I had a powerful experience when he sent energy to my body. I felt a warm, melting sensation as blockages opened and life energy began to flow. I wanted to learn more about this Spring Forest Qigong! Master Lin also asked talked to me about my fear. He said to me, "There is conflict in the world, just as there is cancer in the body, but there is so much more peace. We can think about the conflict but why not think about the peace?" His words were beautiful and comforting.

Doing the Qigong exercises has really helped me to get back in touch with my whole being and nurture myself. Could it be that sometimes we just really forget how to breath...how to draw in the energy of the universe...to commune with our Maker and appreciate all that surrounds us? I understand fully how blockages are created in the body and see how our culture fosters illness, especially cancer. We are exposed to so many things in our environment and our lifestyles are often filled with activities and stress. It only makes sense that if we have blockages - physical and emotional - illness will develop.

The beauty of the Spring Forest Qigong is the gentleness and ease that it can be incorporated into your life. Making time to do the exercises is making time for your spirit - and truly integrating the mind, body & spirit necessary for healing. "Simple, but profound"...a perfect description for Spring Forest Qigong.

I took Level 1 & 2 classes from Master Lin and learned a great deal. He is a wonderful teacher and his life experiences are very moving. I know I'm a different person since my introduction to Spring Forest Qigong and Master Lin. I'm calmer and more centered. I'm more sure of myself and less concerned with myself! I certainly move through the world differently...more at peace...more with the flow than against it. I share my understanding of Qi and its flow with our two horses and others on the farm, often able to sense when they need some of my energy. And, I always get back more from our encounters!

I have remained cancer-free for the last 2-1/2 years and will continue to practice Spring Forest Qigong for the rest of my years here on earth. It's become a form of meditation and prayer and I trust that it's making a difference in my life. I feel blessed to have traveled the path of my life's journey and so lucky that it led to Master Lin.

ROBIN TROMBLEY
Coon Rapids, MN

Peace of Mind

When my oldest son was 14, in the beginning of his freshman year in high school, a classmate of his brought assorted fireworks to school. My son set off a smoke bomb and eventually was expelled from the entire school district.

Once he was expelled from school he started running away from home. Basically, I was a basket case. I was delivering Meals on Wheels one day, listening to KFAI. On Tuesday's they have a program called "The Inner Journey." Chunyi was a guest on the show and I found it fascinating, listening to him speak. Even though I was delivering meals, I didn't want to leave the car. I wanted to stay and listen to his every word.

Chunyi mentioned that he was offering classes at Anoka-Ramsey Community college. I jotted down the phone number and I thought this would be doable, since the College is near my home. When I arrived home from work, there was an article in the newspaper about Qigong and also a piece of mail that had come from an HMO and Qigong was mentioned in that article. I'd never heard of Qigong before and I received three messages in one day. So, I said to myself "I know I'm thick, but I get it."

I signed up for the next session of Level I. I found that when I began practicing the active exercises, the more I practiced, the less my son ran away. Qigong helped me to not obsess when he would run away. It gave me my sanity.

Qigong has allowed me to let go. It helped me to let go of the fear, anxiety, apprehension, the desire to control, all

247

of that.

And, it's also helped in other relationships, especially, in my work relationships. I work with 460 volunteers, 200 clients and there is a great deal of interaction with people. Many of these people have health issues and other problems in their lives. You come across people who are angry or are difficult to deal with and Qigong has helped in effectively working with these people, too.

Sometimes, I think in contact or conversation with others, you can see a change in their behavior reflected by your behavior. Specifically, being proactive instead of reactive.

Before I would tense up and feel very uncomfortable. I used to have a tough time dealing with conflict. I'm a procrastinator, Qigong has helped with that, too. You know, when stuff happens, just dealing with it. It doesn't have to be a big deal. It doesn't have to be a conflict.

I think Spring Forest Qigong had everything to do with the aforementioned, because no other changes have occurred in my life.

If it weren't for Spring Forest Qigong I don't know what events would have transpired, but they wouldn't have been good. I'm sure I would have suffered some type of illness from all the stress.

When I think of Spring Forest Qigong my first thought is peace of mind.

ESTHER TREJO
St. Paul, MN

Lung Disease

I have what they call viliar protinosis. What happens is protein builds up in the air sacks in your lungs. Once that protein builds up it's like sand. Of course, when your air sacks are filled up with sand that's going to cause you a lot of problems like not being able to breathe, gasping for air.

I was diagnosed with this disease 17 years ago and went on oxygen 24 hours a day. Everywhere I went I was attached to an oxygen canister that I would roll around on wheels. It was so bad that sometimes I didn't think I would make it just for the short time it took to change from one canister to the next.

The doctors told me the only way I was ever going to get off oxygen was to have a lung transplant. I had been to the Mayo Clinic and they told me that and my St. Paul lung doctor also told me the same thing. I really did not want to go that route. I did not feel it was right that someone else would have to die so I could get their lungs so I could live. I just had trouble handling that concept of a lung transplant.

I was on oxygen 24 hours a day from November of 1986 until March of 1993. I have not had a lung transplant and yet I am no longer on oxygen. The reason is that I met Chunyi Lin.

He was teaching at class at night at a local high school on something called Qigong. My son, Ralph, found out about Mr. Lin's class and told me I should go. My son said he believed Mr. Lin could help me. I did not believe he could and I did not want to go. I just thought there's no way that's gonna help. No way. My son wouldn't stop insisting and I was almost dragged kicking and screaming to the first class.

I didn't want to be there and I just sat and glared at Mr. Lin the whole time. But, there was something so gentle and loving about him I decided to go back the next week. I went to the class every week and learned to do his exercises. I started feeling better and just kept getting better and better.

I guess it was the fifth or sixth week of class I walked in without using the oxygen. For awhile I kept carrying it as a safety precaution so I had it with me. So, I go to class, I'm the first one there. And as everybody filed in they kept saying, "Esther, where's your oxygen?!" No one could believe it and Master Lin walks in and he looks at me and everybody was so happy. They were just in awe. They just couldn't believe it. Everybody was just ecstatic. It was a miracle!

By the last week of class I walked in without oxygen at all. It was the first time I had been off the oxygen for more than six years. I've been off ever since. Every year now I celebrate on March 22nd my Freedom from Oxygen Day. My doctor just couldn't figure it out.

I mean I thank God that there was oxygen for me to survive all those years while I was on it, but I was only surviving. I was alive but I wasn't living.

I thank God every day for Master Lin. He gave me a whole quality of life and I think that's what we all want. I continued to study with Master Lin and have gone through Level III of Spring Forest Qigong. And, I've been able to help several of my friends with health problems using what Master Lin has taught me. I have three triplet grandchildren. They're almost six years old now and I know without Master Lin I probably wouldn't have lived to see them.

Knowing him has changed my life in so many ways. I'm also a different person because of what I've learned from him. To put it bluntly, I used to be a real judgmental, crabby S.O.B. but because of Spring Forest Qigong I'm not any more. I have a lot of love and understanding of the world and of people and for that I'm very thankful and Master Lin is the reason why.

Master Lin was here at my house for Christmas and my little grandson, one of the triplets, said to him as he was leaving, "Are you Jesus?"

We all got a big chuckle out of that. Well, I don't think he's Jesus, of course, but he is Jesus' helper. Certainly, he's here on earth to help us.

KATHY WEIHE
Little Canada, MN

Multiple Sclerosis (MS)

I took Spring Forest Qi-gong, level 1, when I was forty-one years old.

At that time, I was in the middle of a divorce and living with my teenaged son and daughter. I had been diagnosed with multiple sclerosis six years earlier, and had lived almost daily with fears of the future and the possibility of increasing symptoms of M.S. All the members of my family were struggling with the pains of a divorce, and my life was in chaos.

When I began studying qi-gong with Master Lin everything, simply and quietly, changed. I looked forward to the early evening, when I closed my bedroom door, repeated the words I learned in class, and practiced the basic movements of qi-gong. In less than half an hour, I felt calmer. My night-time dreaming became vivid and energized, and I looked forward to class meetings, where I could talk about practicing level 1.

Fatigue was my predominant M.S. symptom; I had been wary of taking the class at night, afraid that I might get too tired from driving through January weather for forty minutes to the community college. However, my energy level improved, becoming more constant and steady, and I worried much less about what I could or could not do with my body.

Within the six weeks of the level 1 class, I experienced strong physical changes, as well as some shifts in my feelings about time (specifically, that I needed to be in no rush to heal). The next time Master Lin offered classes, I signed up for level 2.

As my energy level rose, so did my confidence. Once, when I expressed fear about something to Master Lin, he told me to have confidence. "Have confidence." As if he were offering me a cookie from a tray, which I could just take up and eat. And he was. Confidence is a form of energy, and I was learning from Qigong how to use the energy around me. I started to trust my ability to be active without becoming overly tired, and to believe that tiredness was nothing to fear.

My confidence increased dramatically by the summer after my first classes in Spring Forest Qi-gong. My friends have to remind me of my life before studying with Mr. Lin, when I would not walk around the lake, or attend more than one event in a day without fear about my health.

I took up rock-climbing, a sport which had interested me since I was a girl, and traveled to several states on climbing trips. I applied for an MFA program and attended graduate school in the fall. By the following January, I was able to travel to and explore the rain forest in Costa Rica, all the while keeping up my daily practice of Qigong

I have studied Spring Forest Qigong through level 4, learning more about working on other people to help open up their blockages. At first, I thought I could not help someone else, since I did not have perfect health myself; I have learned from Master Lin and fellow students that this is not true. It has been almost seven years since I first heard about Qigong from a woman at my church. I approached her about this thing she talked about —Qigong -- because she seemed "radiantly healthy," and happy. I found out she had begun her study of the moving meditation when she'd had cancer.

I still practice Qigong every night, mostly through the

sitting meditations. Sometimes, when I feel the need to, I go back to the first comforting movements of level 1. I "think Qigong" while I drive my car or sit at my desk or load the dishwasher, especially when I feel tired. My health has been good. Thanks to Master Lin, I don't think of myself as someone who has an illness, but rather as someone who can pay attention to blockages in my body and work to open them.

My spiritual life is very important to me. Qigong is an active part of that life. For me, the basic movements of Qigong are moving prayer. I no longer fear as much for the future, for myself or the people I love. Master Lin's answering machine used to end with the message, "Have a nice and lucky day." I've had many of them since I met Chunyi and started studying Spring Forest Qigong.

Closing Thoughts

If you never heard of Qigong before reading this book, I hope you have a better understanding now of what Qigong offers you.

There are many aspects to Qigong. Many people see Qigong as a fitness and wellness program. Indeed, practicing Qigong is an excellent program for fitness and wellness.

Qigong breathing increases the intake of oxygen and greatly enhances the metabolism of oxygen in the tissues of the body, especially the muscles. Physically, this helps give you more strength and endurance. It also makes you more mentally alert and enhances creativity.

Qigong meditation relieves stress, which is one of the major causes of disease. It also slows the heart rate and respiration. It strengthens the immune system. When you do meditation, your brain sends chemical messages to your body to help you relax. It also enhances an over all feeling of well-being.

Practicing Qigong can help you in so many ways. It can help you to achieve your "peak performance" in sports, at school, at work and in life. You mind is more alert and creative. Your muscles are more relaxed and strengthened. You have more energy. For these reasons alone it is easy to see why Qigong is becoming so popular.

There is also another dimension to Qigong which I have focused on in this book - healing. Many Qigong masters do not focus on this in their teaching. As a result, many students of Qigong are not even aware of this dimension of Qigong. I feel healing is the most important.

Learning and practicing Spring Forest Qigong is an excellent fitness and wellness program and it focuses on the healing power of Qigong. Spring Forest Qigong can help you take control of your own health. It can help you to heal physically, mentally, emotionally and spiritually, all at the same time. And, you can learn to help others to heal as well.

I began this book by saying that you were born a healer. I believe this to be true because I know it to be true. I hope this book has helped you to have a better understanding of how Qigong works and how you can use the Qi, the energy, of love, kindness and forgiveness to bring about your own complete and perfect healing and to help others.

When a person always has love, forgiveness and kindness in their heart, happiness is always with them and their energy channels are always open. If a blockage does occur for some reason, it is so easy to get rid of.

In my experience, Qigong is one of the most powerful healing techniques ever developed. However, Qigong is not the fountain of youth or the gift of immortality. Those things do not exist. We are all here for a limited time. We come from the universe. We are part of the universe and we will go back to the universe.

The most important thing is how we spend our time in this body and how we grow in the energy of love, kindness and forgiveness. This is what makes our life most enjoyable and wonderful.

My only goal is to share this wonderful message with as many people as possible. I hope that you will give Spring Forest Qigong a try and choose to join me in my vision of "a healer in every family and a world without pain."

To learn more about Spring Forest Qigong and the learning materials we have available, please visit our websites at:

www.springforestqigong.com
&
www.bornahealer.com

Research on Spring Forest Qigong

In China, many fine Qigong Masters have no interest in research projects. After all there are thousands of years of Qigong research to draw upon and they have years of their own personal experience with what works and what doesn't.

Living in America I have learned the value people place on scientific studies which is why I am very open to them. I have been working for several years with a highly respected medical researcher to gain funding for a study using Spring Forest Qigong to help cancer patients. Such studies are expensive and we are still seeking funding.

In 2002, a research project was completed studying the use of Spring Forest Qigong in helping people with severe depression and bipolar disorder. The following is an overview of that study.

Spring Forest Qigong found "highly effective"in treating Depression

A study conducted during the summer of 2002 found that Spring Forest Qigong "is a highly effective complementary and alternative treatment modality for depression and should be considered as an adjunct to psychotherapy treatment."

The study was conducted over a period of two months by Frances V. Gaik, a doctoral candidate at the Adler School of Psychology in Chicago, Illinois. The findings were included in Ms. Gaik's dissertation. She subsequently was awarded her doctorate in January of 2003.

After in depth research into qigong techniques, Dr. Gaik selected Spring Forest Qigong techniques for her study. A total of "39 subjects suffering from DSM-IV diagnosis of Major Depressions, Dysthymia or Bipolar Disorder" were taught the Level One Spring Forest Qigong techniques by Master Chunyi Lin in a one-day training session at the end of June 2002. Master Lin met with the subjects again at the end of July and the end of August.

Each subject was also provided with a SFQ Level One videotape, manual and audiotapes including the SFQ Small Universe and Self-Concentration meditations. The subjects were directed to practice either the Level One Active Exercises or meditations for at least forty minutes each day and to keep a log of their practice sessions.

Dr. Gaik found that "all subjects improved over the treatment period" and found "a very significant level of improvement in the majority of the subjects who were measured at serious levels of depression."

The following are excerpts from Dr. Gaik's study: "A Preliminary Study Applying Spring Forest Qigong to Depression as an Alternative and Complementary Treatment."

ABSTRACT

A pilot study with 39 subjects suffering from DSM-IV diagnosis of Major Depression, Dysthymia or Bipolar Disorder were treated with the Eastern Traditional Chinese Medicine technique of qigong. Treatment included qi emission treatment by qualified practitioners, and subjects were required to practice qigong exercise for a two-month period. Significant improvement was observed, especially in the first month on the measurements of Beck's Depression Index-Revised (BDI-R) (.0000) and Symptom Checklist -90 R (SCL-90-R) Depression Index (.00003), Interpersonal Sensitivity (.00003). SCL-90 Somaticism indexes as well as three criteria from DSM-IV guidelines are also reported on indicating an overall trend of improvement over time. All subjects improved over the treatment period and it is determined that the qigong exercise is a highly effective complementary and alternative treatment modality for depression and should be considered as an adjunct to psychotherapy treatment. No significant difference was seen in those subjects treated with qi emission.

Anecdotal Reports

Specific reports of somatic and symptom relief were reported which deserve to be mentioned: 1) one woman stated that the ringing in her ear had disappeared immediately after the first qi emission treatment. She reported that she had consistently experienced this ringing for a period of nine years; 2) another woman stated that she had reduced her insulin levels; 3) another woman with numerous physical problems stated that she no longer needed to take Vicodin to sleep at night, and she began a job after a long period of not working; 4) another woman stated she had cut her anti-depressant medication in half; 5) another woman stated that she found she could get answers to her problems while doing the qigong exercise.

("A Preliminary Study Applying Spring Forest Qigong to Depression as an Alternative and Complementary Treatment," Frances V. Gaik, Psy. D. pg. 81)

Research Results

The results were most successful in that the subjects reported significant and substantial relief of symptoms connected with DSM-IV guidelines and there were no reported negative side effects of the treatment.

The researcher and all three practitioners noted that physical presentation and appearance of the group was markedly different and improved at the end of the treatment period than when they first presented two months earlier. There was a noticeable difference in the affect and presentation of the subjects. The practitioners commented on their original concern at the first meeting about how "serious" and sad the subjects looked. By the last session, the subjects displayed an enthusiastic attitude and their affect was markedly changed to a more responsive and animated level. They were genuinely curious about the qigong technique and made inquiry about advanced levels of practice. Although the study treatment period lasted only two months, the trend of improvement may continue to be experienced with continuation of the exercise as length of practice indicates that greater change can occur over time, especially after 12 months (Kawano, 1997; 1998).

(Ibid. pg. 83)

Clinical Implications

The health care system is currently in a state of crisis with more than 41 million people uninsured and mental health care is, in reality, a non-issue with insurance carriers. The current accepted mode of treatment for depression, the most commonly diagnosed mental difficulty, includes cognitive behavioral therapy and medication. The perspective that we are interconnected through an energy field and that this energy can be enhanced and ultimately exchanged in human interactions, whether they be through thoughts, emotions or physical action, is a major shift in paradigm which is not addressed in the current accepted therapies. The qigong exercise is believed to enhance the human energy system of the individual over time, building upon health and a sense of well being. According to qigong principles, the individual subjects learned to cultivate, store and manipulate "energy" or qi which activated symptom relief. The subjects could indeed have learned to mobilize innate healing potential and reverse the negative effects of depression, as well as taking personal responsibility for their health.

An energetic approach to depression offers the opportunity to change our perception about human relationships and how to modulate our own response to "toxic environments" and their effects upon our own energy field. The subjects in this study were not removed from their everyday difficulties, nor were they given psychotherapy; they were trained in how to better cope with and balance their emotional world and to develop a sense of self mastery. A balanced control of their response was the goal rather than a dependency upon medication or the need to see a therapist.

This is the first study to apply qigong as a curative in depression and significant results were observed over the short-term of two months. The subjects learned a technique which offers a lifetime modality for dealing with stress and the negative effects of depression. If the trend continues as expected, they may have learned to mobilize their own healing potential. The technique is cost effective (the price of the video and audio tapes) and there were no reported side effects of the exercise.

The results provided a significant improvement in all subjects. In applications of a new treatment, only a few events of sufficiently high significance can be enough to assert that a new phenomenon exists with a high level of confidence; this study indicates a very significant level of improvement in the majority of the subjects who were measured at serious levels of depression. The qigong exercise has been differentiated from meditation and visualization through EEG activity (Ueda, et. Al.,1997), which cannot merely account for the significant levels of improvement seen in this study. The qigong exercise is not comparable to physical exercise, in that it is not exertive to the levels necessary to release endorphins.

Given the theoretical acceptance of the concept that the human system has energy transformers called chakras and that we are affected by the flow of this energy through the meridian system, speculation on the results may be considered in light of energetic theories posited by Kunz and Peper (1983). Dora Kunz was one of the originators of Therapeutic Touch which is widely taught and used by nursing staff.

A decrease of energy is a common factor of depression and there are complex factors involved. Normal mood changes of anxiety, disappointment and sadness may be an incipient factor in shutting down or closing of the solar plexus chakra, responsible for the main energy flow intake, according to Kunz. As the whole system is energetically recharging at a lower rate, the individual is expending more energy through dealing with turbulent feelings, and consequently less energy is available. Anxious and depressed individuals tend to breathe in a shallow pattern, and this will also affect the flow of oxygen and energy into the body. The qigong exercise encourages a deep and measured breath, increasing oxygen to the organism.

(ibid. pg 87-89)

For more information on Dr. Gaik's study "A Preliminary

Study Applying Spring Forest Qigong to Depression as an Alternative and Complementary Treatment" contact the Adler School of Professional Psychology *where her complete research results and dissertation are on file.*

Adler School of Professional Psychology
65 East Wacker Place, Suite 2100
Chicago, Illinois 60601-7298
ph: (312) 201-5900
fax: (312) 201-5917
email: information@adler.edu

Coauthor's Notes

Someone asked me recently how I came to believe that Spring Forest Qigong actually works. It's a question I've been asked many times. The short answer is slowly and reluctantly. Only after many months of careful research did I accept the possibility that it could work.

For most of my adult life I have been a professional skeptic – a reporter. I've spent thirty years in the TV news business. It was in that capacity I first became aware of Chunyi Lin and Spring Forest Qigong in the late fall of 1996 while working as an anchor and reporter for KMSP-TV in Minneapolis.

A couple people I knew were taking one of his classes and couldn't stop talking about it. They raved about the "healing energy" and how people's pain was miraculously going away and how they could "feel the energy surging" through them. While the sincerity in their enthusiasm was obviously real, it struck me as fanciful at best and perhaps delusional.

I had never heard of such a thing before; "an unlimited source of energy that flows throughout the universe" and flows through these invisible channels in our bodies. The whole concept seemed absurd. I knew what energy was. Energy is what flows along power lines and lights up the room when you flip the switch.

This certainly wasn't the first time I'd encountered something that sounded too good to be true. In my personal and professional experience such claims usually turned out to be overblown and sometimes fraudulent.

We all view life through the prism of our own experi-

265

ences. That is what provides us with perspective and context for learning and understanding. We are subjective in our thought processes. True objectivity is a laudable goal but nearly impossible to achieve. While I strive to be an open-minded skeptic, my skepticism about Qigong was fueled in part by my past experiences.

During the twelve years I lived and worked in San Francisco I knew a lot of people who raved about other unconventional concepts that I considered to be from a similar vein as what I was being told about Qigong; everything from EST to TM to Rolfing to isolation tanks. The enthusiasm of those individuals was equally sincere and often intense but usually faded or disappeared entirely within a relatively brief passage of time.

Being an open-minded skeptic, I was often intrigued enough by the possibilities these concepts proffered that I experimented with many of them. However, none ever resonated with me. I received no perceivable benefit from any of them. Therefore, as far as I was concerned, the claims were false. Perhaps the failure was totally mine or just in my skeptical approach. Still, my experiences with all of the things I had tried from that genre were in stark contrast to the "enlightening" experiences others alleged. My experiences were pedestrian not profound. As a consequence, it was through the prism of those experiences I viewed what I was hearing about Qigong.

I might have dismissed Qigong entirely save for the fact that as a reporter I was as curious as I was skeptical, perhaps even more so. Qigong could turn out to be a good story, providing I could find any proof to support the claims. Conversely, if I could disprove them, that could be an even better story.

Several months passed before I found the time to start

investigating Qigong. Once I did, to my great surprise, I rather quickly discovered there had been a great deal of scientific research conducted on the subject. Most of the research was from China and Japan where the concept of Qi, or Ki, as they say it in Japan, are part of the culture.

I quickly discovered that in China the concept of "Qi cultivation" or Qigong dates back at least four thousand years. Qi cultivation is the foundation of all traditional Chinese medicine including acupuncture, which had already become accepted by many in the Western world. Facts you have, no doubt, already learned from this book.

During the era of Mao Tse Tung's rule over China, Qigong was forced underground. Qigong empowers the individual, which put at it odds with the collective, state-centered mentally of Mao's government. Mao saw it as a potential threat. It wasn't until after Mao's death and the removal of his closest followers from the halls of power that Qigong began to reemerge.

In the early 1980's, a highly respected Chinese medical doctor persuaded the new communist government that the ancient healing tradition could prove to be of great benefit to the people. With the new leaders focusing on modernizing China, the doctor was allowed to examine Qigong healing techniques through the lens of modern scientific doctrine. They wanted hard evidence and to my great surprise they had gotten it.

Since the 1980's, scores of Qigong studies have been conducted in China. The results are voluminous. The sheer numbers are impressive. However, the research techniques used have not always met Western standards leading some to question those results. Still, enough of the Chinese studies have been considered scientifically solid that interest in Qigong is growing among researchers in the West.

The Chinese government has still not openly embraced Qigong but apparently some government leaders have found the research results persuasive enough to stop suppressing Qigong teaching and practice. In fact, Qigong healing techniques are now allowed to be used openly in some of the nation's hospitals.

While I encourage everyone to do their own research and come to their own conclusions, what follows is a very condensed version of some of what I discovered. I offer it only as a brief explanation of how my thinking on the subject progressed and changed.

In my mind, for Qigong to hold the possibility of any efficacy, there would have to be some hard evidence proving that this energy or meridian system, which is supposed to facilitate the flow of Qi in the body, exists. I strongly doubted such a thing could be proven. I soon discovered I was wrong.

By the mid-1990's, the Qi cultivation discipline that had been studied most outside of China was acupuncture. Many of these acupuncture studies did withstand Western scrutiny and demonstrated conclusively that the energy system or meridians in the body do indeed exist. I even found a number of medical doctors, including some in the Twin Cities where I lived and worked, who participated in acupuncture studies in medical school and found the technique very impressive.

In a typical acupuncture study, researchers would inject a tracer or radio-isotope into an energy point along a specific meridian system or channel in a subject's body as directed by a skilled acupuncturist. The purpose was to see if the tracer would move and if it did, would it move along the meridians or channels as they appear on a classic meridian chart. Time and time again, they found the tracer would immediately flow along that same, specific, meridian channel where the tracer had been injected.

The researchers also found if they injected the tracer even slightly outside of a specific energy point, all the tracer did was pool in that spot. It went nowhere. These results clearly demonstrated the existence of a system of otherwise invisible meridians or channels within the human body, just as Eastern scholars had been teaching for many millennia. Here was proof of a system that was previously unrecognized and unknown to modern medicine. I found that to be truly astounding.

Furthermore, theses studies were not conducted just in China and Japan but also in Europe and even here in the United States including the highly regarded Menninger Foundation. The studies were significant enough that some insurance companies began covering acupuncture treatments and most do today.

The findings of those acupuncture studies were extremely surprising to me personally as well as professionally. Years earlier, I had tried acupuncture treatments in hopes of relieving my chronic, progressive back pain and received no benefit from them at all. The studies I was reviewing stood in stark contrast to my personal experience and beliefs. Consequently, my mind became more open to the possibilities of Qigong, my skepticism began to wane and my curiosity grew intensely.

The evidence was quite clear that this energy meridian system within the human body does exist. Therefore, it was only logical to assume it also served some purpose. As Albert Einstein once said, "God does not roll dice with the universe." Continuing that line of thinking a step further, it became logical to me that if the energy system exists then the energy – the Qi – might also exist. Something must move along those meridians.

To my mind these studies provided scientific validation of a key part of the ancient concept behind Qigong. However, they only proved the energy system could be manipulated by a skilled technician using acupuncture needles, nothing else.

As I continued to speak with doctors and other researchers interested in Qigong, I was made aware of numerous studies that focused on the manipulation of Qi without needles or any other implement. Studies using Kirlian photography and infrared thermovision had generated images of what was purported to be Qi energy and documented that a Qigong master can increase the Qi in his own body and send Qi out from his body.

Other research indicated that emitted Qi can increase the count of T-cells in the body, reduce and even eliminate tumors in the body and effect the growth of cancer cells. I did not then and still do not possess the requisite scientific knowledge base to fairly evaluate the significance of any of those findings but they did encourage me to keep looking.

Eventually, I discovered two studies on Qi manipulation that I did find compelling. Each of these studies focused on what the researchers called "synchronicity." These were double blind studies that measured the changes in the EEGs, or brain waves, of a Qigong master to the brain waves of the recipients of the master's Qi.

There was no way for the recipients or the researchers with them to know when the master was sending Qi and when he wasn't. Yet, the studies found synchronization of EEGs between the sender and the recipients of the Qi.

Whenever the master sent out his Qi, within seconds the brain waves of the recipients changed and became synchronized with those of the master. When he stopped sending Qi, the synchronicity stopped.

In one of the studies the sender and receiver were not only in separate rooms but on separate floors of a sensory-shielded building. The Qigong master was in a room on the fourth floor while the subject was in a room on the first floor. Once again, the data showed that when the Qigong master was sending out Qi the alpha waves in the frontal and occipital lobes of the recipient synchronized with that of the master.

The odds against that happening time and time again by mere coincidence are astronomical. The implication was undeniable. These researchers had documented energy transference. That isn't supposed to be possible. Here was something that cannot be seen somehow moving from one human being through his intent to another human being instantaneously and having a perceivable effect. Think about the implications of that for a minute.

The more I thought about that and all I'd learned I found myself led to the following conclusions: Qi does exist; the energy system for moving Qi through the body does exist; and Qi can be manipulated by human beings.

I had become satisfied that the basic tenets of Qigong were indeed fact not fiction and decided that a report on Qigong would not only be a good story but also a valuable one. Here was something that could actually make a positive difference in people's lives.

I contacted Chunyi Lin and scheduled a time to come to one of his classes and conduct an interview. While I did not mention it in my news report and have seldom mentioned it to anyone prior to writing this, when I first met

Chunyi I was struck most by how comforting it felt to be in his presence.

I had only met two other people in my life who made me feel that way. Both were nuns in the Philippines who had devoted their lives to helping the poor and did so at great personal risk because their work and outspoken drive to put an end to unnecessary suffering had put them at odds with the brutal Marcos dictatorship. To get that same feeling from Chunyi Lin had a profound and puzzling effect on me.

My personal reaction aside, there were two factors that shaped my professional opinion of Chunyi Lin more than any others. First, he is totally unassuming. He didn't want and would not accept credit for the results people were experiencing. He made it very clear the healing came from the universe, from God, from the energy, but not from Chunyi Lin.

Secondly, he insisted that anyone and everyone could do what he was doing, if they only knew how. All he wanted to do was pass on this knowledge to others so they could do the same.

We aired my piece about Chunyi Lin and Spring Forest Qigong at the end of June, 1997. The response was immediate and overwhelming. Something I never would have anticipated.

In my experience only stories that outraged people ever generated much of a response. People love positive stories but they seldom get people excited enough to pick up a phone. To my surprise I never got a negative call about that story. People just called wanting to know how to contact Chunyi Lin and where they could sign up for his classes. And they called in throngs.

I got so many calls I put the number for Anoka-Ramsey

College, where Chunyi was teaching, on my answering machine. I later learned from the college that their phone system had been swamped. They didn't keep an exact tally but it was something like seventeen-hundred calls in ten days. They got so many calls that much of the time their system couldn't handle them all. As a result they had no idea how many people actually tried to call, but they'd never experienced anything like it before or since. The number of people enrolling in his classes increased ten-fold from that day on.

Even after all the research I'd done, even after all the interviews with Chunyi's students and their doctors documenting some truly amazing success stories, I never thought about putting Qigong to use for myself. Looking back on it, I suppose I figured all those people must have had some special quality that enables Qigong to work for them. A quality I was certain I did not possess.

At that point in my life I had suffered from progressive lower back pain for nearly twenty years. About every six months my back problems would become so severe my back would just totally lock up requiring some serious pharmaceutical assistance.

One time my back locked up while I was bent over raking in my yard. The muscles went into such total spasm they were like knotted iron. I couldn't straighten up. I looked like a standing L and the pain was extraordinary. It shot through me like electric shocks with the slightest movement.

There was no way I could drive. I couldn't even manage the two steps to get back into my house to use the phone. Fortunately for me there was a hospital just the other side of the hill from my house. So, using the rake I had in my hand as a crutch, I shuffled like the thousand year old man the four blocks to John Muir Hospital, down my hill, up the next hill and down the other side to the Emergency Room.

That wasn't the worst episode I ever had but it's one of the few I can look back on and laugh about. I must have been quite a sight, bent in two, covered in dirt and sweat, shuffling along with a garden rake.

Drugs and surgery were all the doctors had to offer. The problem was, if I took enough dope to really deal with the pain, I was too spaced out to function. I'd heard too many horror stories about complications from back surgery to even consider that route.

Advil helped more than anything else and I took a dozen or more a day. I tried all kinds of doctors and therapists and chiropractors. Some of the chiropractic treatments actually helped quite a bit. Unfortunately, the relief never lasted more than a few hours or a day at most. Then the pain would come creeping back. In those days even that seemed like a miracle. Like most folks with chronic pain or back problems I'd just learned to live with it and some days were better than others.

A couple of months after the story on Chunyi was broadcast he asked me to help him make a videotape so people could learn his level one exercises at home. I was flattered to be asked and happy to help.

While I'd watched people do the exercises while working on the news piece, I hadn't learned how to perform them myself. It wasn't necessary to do the story. Now, I needed to know, if I was going to produce an instructional video that was worthwhile.

Over the next few weeks I spent a lot of time talking with Chunyi about how Qigong really works and learning how to do the active exercises; one on one instruction that provided me valuable insights into the man and his teachings. The first time I put all the level one exercises together and did them by myself it took about a half an hour and didn't really feel like much. My back still hurt when I was through. I noticed that.

When I awakened the next day, my whole body hurt. I couldn't understand it. The exercises aren't at all strenuous. When I was younger I used to compete in martial arts. I had been a power lifter. I had experienced a lot of injuries and muscle pain. This made no sense. I figured I must be getting the flu or something so I didn't do the active exercises that day.

A couple days later I felt better so I tried the active exercises again and the following day the same thing happened. I hurt all over. This time I called Chunyi. When I told him what I was experiencing, he was very excited and said, "That's good." I replied, "No, that's bad. I feel worse not better."

Chunyi just chuckled and told me that I had blockages that been in place for many years and they were opening up very fast which was very positive. He told me to keep doing the active exercises every day for five days in a row and see what happened.

If I hadn't had such positive feelings about Chunyi as a person, I probably wouldn't have done it. I reluctantly agreed and spent thirty minutes a day practicing those movements for five consecutive days. On the sixth day I was really busy and I was halfway through the day before it dawned on me I didn't hurt anymore. My back didn't even hurt. I could move. I could bend. There was no more pain. Now, I was a believer.

Another year would pass before I actually tried using the Spring Forest Qigong techniques to help others. It might never have happened if my then nine-year-old son hadn't begged me to try it when he got really sick to his stomach late one night. "Do that China stuff, Dad. Make it stop." He'd taken some medicine a few hours early with no relief. It was just getting worse. The poor little guy hurt so much he was in tears.

I didn't think there was any way I could help but I couldn't just walk out of the room and leave him. So, I finally said, "Okay, Buddy, we're going to make that pain go away right now. You just close your eyes." I said a silent prayer – a plea for help really – and did exactly what Chunyi had taught me. It took no longer than a few minutes and just like that his pain went away, the knot in his stomach disappeared, his body relaxed and he fell right to sleep.

Not until that moment did I fully comprehend what Chunyi Lin had told me the first time I met him. Anybody and everybody can use this healing energy to help themselves and others. I'm no longer surprised that Qigong helps people but I'm still amazed by it.

Since Chunyi and I started working together on this book and some other projects about two years ago, I've done a lot more research into Qigong. I've also interviewed literally hundreds of Spring Forest Qigong students. So far, I haven't met a single one who's had a negative experience. Maybe it's the reporter in me but I've found that surprising.

Not everyone has achieved the results they were hoping for but I've yet to meet anyone who's actually practiced the techniques who hasn't had a really positive experience. Many times it's much different than what they were anticipating. For some, for most actually, it's been more positive than they ever believed possible and they speak of Spring Forest Qigong and Chunyi Lin in the most glowing terms.

Over the past few years I've spent a considerable amount of time with Chunyi Lin, observed him in many different situations and have gotten to know him pretty well. I know him to be a gifted teacher and healer and a truly loving and giving man. He is just as unassuming and totally focused on helping others today as he was the first time I met him. Put simply, he's the real deal. He lives what he teaches and leads by example. In my experience those qualities are far too rare.

My heartfelt thanks and gratitude to the scores and scores of Spring Forest Qigong students who have so generously given of their time to speak with me and so openly shared their stories and often the intimate details of their lives in the desire to help others. Without them this book would not have been possible.

It is a pleasure and privilege to call Chunyi Lin my friend and I am honored to have the opportunity to work with him and so many other kind, loving and giving individuals on a project that offers so much help to so many.

About the Authors

Chunyi Lin is a certified International Qigong Master and the creator of Spring Forest Qigong. His fluency in numerous Chinese dialects provided him the rare opportunity to study with many of the most respected Qigong Masters in his native China. He has been teaching Qigong and using Qigong techniques to help others for more than twenty years. Master Lin is also a Tai Chi Master and highly skilled in Chinese herbal medicine and acupuncture.

Mr. Lin served as Director of Qigong Programs at Anoka-Ramsey Community College in Anoka, Minnesota, from 1999 to 2004. During 2004 he created an Educational Partnership with Normandale Community College of Bloomington, MN and his corporate entity, Spring Forest Qigong Co., Inc., to provide fully accredited courses in Spring Forest Qigong health and healing techniques. All of the course curricula were created by Mr. Lin and he serves as the program director and lead instructor. Lin was formerly a college professor in Guangdon Province in China. In January of 2005, Lin received a master's degree in Human Development/ Holistic Health & Wellness from St. Mary's University.

Master Lin teaches four levels of Spring Forest Qigong and has created a series of home learning materials for students, including videos, guided audio meditations and reference manuals. He is a frequent keynote speaker at national health conferences.

Since coming to the United States in 1995, he has helped thousands and thousands of people to learn about the powerful, healing benefits of Spring Forest Qigong. He now devotes all of his time to the teaching of Spring Forest Qigong and helping others. He also sees people for private healing sessions. He lives with his wife and two children in the Twin Cities.

His vision is "a healer in every family and a world without pain."

Gary Rebstock is a thirty year veteran of television news as an anchor, reporter and producer. He has received numerous broadcast journalism awards from regional Emmys to international film festival honors to the Thomas Moore Stork Award for Excellence in International Journalism form the World Affairs Council of San Francisco. He has been a student of Spring Forest Qigong since 1997. He lives in the Twin Cities with his teenage son. He is always interested in learning about the experiences of Spring Forest Qigong students. You can contact him by email at: gary@bornahealer.com.